RV Rentals

A Vacationer's Guide

Dave & Kay Corby

Outskirts Press, Inc.
Denver, Colorado

Outskirts Press
http://www.outskirtspress.com

ISBN-10: 1-59800-179-5
ISBN-13: 978-1-59800-179-2

Library of Congress Control Number 2005935757

Outskirts Press and the "OP" logo are trademarks belonging to
Outskirts Press, Inc.

Printed in the United States of America

"All things considered, there are only two kinds of men in the world – those that stay at home and those that do not. The second are the most interesting."

Rudyard Kipling

Disclaimers & Disclosures

Those who seek the familiar and predictable are perhaps best served by staying home. Travel, at least in part, is a search for the unknown and unexpected. Self-contained, self-guided, self-structured travel – specifically travel by rental RV – will tend to increase your encounters with both the unknown and the unexpected. Many of these encounters will lead to unforeseen pleasures; a few may produce unsought complications and challenges.

Advance research and adequate planning can do much to reduce the number of unexpected problems you encounter. This book presents guidance with the intention of smoothing out the "rough-spots" and increasing the pleasures in your RV rental vacation. This book cannot guarantee you a trouble free trip.

This book is not intended as a technical reference manual for RV Travelers. Excellent books are available in that subject area (we have listed a few in the Appendix). It is not the authors' intention to make a public display of ignorance by attempting to compete with those books already in print. The fact is the authors were both born with defective mechanical aptitude genes. We are hopelessly out of our element when it comes to understanding, let alone repairing, even the most simple of mechanical devices. In fact, we are generally incapable of giving such devices even that somber, contemplative look which seems a precursor to all serious repair attempts.

Additionally, it is not the purpose of this book to restate all of the information which is currently available to RVers and other travelers. It is our intention to supplement those other texts by providing herein information specifically tailored to the needs of the RV renter. For expanded, general information on the subject of RVing, we refer you to those publications recommended in the Appendix.

More Disclaimers & Disclosures

Before we go any further, there are some compliance issues we need to deal with. We live in an era where all legitimate products (and many which are not so legitimate) come with warning labels. We know our readers expect to find these labels on everything. To avoid disappointment in our readership, we include the following:

WARNING

The practice of RVing may lead to a condition known as **"Hitch Itch"**. Hitch Itch is the common name (there is probably some fancy Latin name, but we couldn't say just what it might be) for a malady which infects many who travel by RV. It can strike at anytime and seems particularly insidious in the spring. Symptoms include a strong, but often nonspecific, urge to hitch up trailer or toad and go somewhere. At its most intense, the condition causes those infected to randomly wander around the house tying down all the loose stuff. They are likely to be found studying road atlases as if they contained the wisdom of the ages (which from our perspective may very well be the case).

The authors were first infected over 50 years ago. We find the disease can flair up both suddenly and without warning. At the base of our driveway is THE ROAD. We have figured out this road leads everywhere. When Hitch Itch symptoms are at their most intense, we can entertain ourselves for an hour or more just gazing in a mindless, unfocused sort of way at THE ROAD trying to decide if we, leaving with our trailer and given a choice, would turn left or right on exiting the driveway.

We place this WARNING here because taking an RV trip dramatically increases your chance for infection. In point of fact, that you are reading this book could mean you already have this often pleasant, but annoyingly persistent, condition. And here is the really sinister aspect of Hitch Itch: all cures are only temporary . . . and all involve starting up the engine and going somewhere.

Consider yourself warned!

Contents

Preface

A family vacation in the late 50's was my introduction to RV travel. Kansas to the West Coast and back. The Grand Canyon, Disneyland, Pismo Beach, the Great Salt Lake, Grand Tetons and Yellowstone! Four people in a 16 foot Shasta (yellow with the really cool silver wings in back), no bathroom, sleeping arrangements a bit cramped . . . and the closest to heaven I had then ever been. Though I suppose I didn't know it at the time, I was hooked!

In the years since I have traveled as a backpacker and a car camper. I have journeyed in Van Conversions, a couple of Class C's and a Class A. I have pulled a 16 foot hybrid trailer, 19 and 30 foot conventional trailers, and – most recently – a 33 foot 5th Wheel. I have journeyed literally thousands of nights as a self-contained traveler. And I've only touched lightly on the list of places I'd like to see, things I'd like to do, experiences I'd like to have.

As an RVer, I have seen many wonderful places I might otherwise have missed. RV owners tend to get out on the road more, to spend more time traveling, than our non-RVing friends. As a group, RVers are drawn to the lifestyle by an itch to travel . . . and then we rationalize: Given that we own our RVs, it isn't much more expensive to go somewhere than to stay home. And it seems wasteful to own an RV and not use it. And, with our RVs, we can go all sorts of wonderful places without ever leaving the comforts of home.

We travel. Our homes stay the same. Our backyards change. Our fifth wheel has a large rear window and trips are headlined by the rear window view – by the changes in our backyard. The sun rises out of a mountain lake or sets into the waters of the Florida Keys; a moon rise over Pikes Peak; wild turkey, deer and elk; sandy beaches and sage brush flats – each has been a feature in our backyard.

Find other backyards, that's our idea. Don't fall into the habit of accepting one just because it happens to be behind the sticks and bricks house. Seek other backyards and take time to know them. To begin to know a place requires we imagine life there, and we find the imagining is not likely to be very tangible until we have actually settled in a spot – even if for a short time.

This is a book for those seeking new backyards.

Dave Corby
Parker, Colorado
June, 2005

Introduction

The words "Let's go RVing" are inherently exciting – an implied adventure in the words "Let's go" and a sense of something fresh with the addition of the idea of "RVing". The thought of traveling in a new way and to new places is exhilarating. Your presence here, in this book, suggests you are at least thinking about a rental RV vacation and that you recognize a need for further knowledge. We congratulate you on your willingness to consider new ways of doing things!

From the perspective of one who has never traveled by RV, we recognize RVs seem large (which is of course true), and generally incomprehensible (which is false). All who now RV have stood where you now stand – in a place of not knowing, of facing discomforting complexity. That millions have stood where you now stand and gone on to have pleasant RV experiences would indicate you are in a perfect place.

People come to this book for a variety of reasons, seeking a wide range of information. Some of you picked up this book from a place of curiosity – you may never have really considered an RV vacation and may be in a very preliminary phase of information gathering. Others will have already made their decision, committed to an RV rental and come to this book simply looking for some last minute tips to make the journey smoother and more enjoyable. Some of you are RVers with years of experience. Others have never even been inside an RV.

$AVING$ TIP$

You Will Read Elsewhere That Vacationing In An RV Is As Much As 70% Cheaper than other means of travel. True enough if you are comparing the cost of an RV vacation to going on a cruise and staying in the ship's penthouse suite, otherwise the notion of 70% savings is total nonsense. On the other hand, properly planned RV Rental vacations do offer opportunities for expense reductions not available in more conventional vacations. Throughout this book we have inserted highlighted boxes like this one to alert you to savings opportunities.

Organization & Objectives

The journey between the RV novice and the seasoned veteran of RV Travel is not as long as it might appear. The path starts with a bit of knowledge and leads to a never ending course of "hands on" learning. This book's function is to provide the introductory knowledge needed to get you on the road. There you will begin your own process of experience gathering.

"RV Rentals" is designed to guide you through your first rental RV vacation. This book is divided into four parts; each part presents a collection of chapters with focus on a particular phase of vacationing in a rental RV. It is not necessary to read this book in the order it is written or to read it from cover-to-cover. Using this summary and the Table of Contents as your guides, go directly to those parts of most immediate importance to you.

PART 1 – DECISIONS, DECISIONS

In this section we introduce the RV lifestyle and help you make the important, upfront decisions which are the foundation of an enjoyable RV vacation.

The first two chapters will provide an overview. In **Chapter 1, "Why Rent an RV?"** we introduce you to the kind of folks who RV and to the sorts of reasons which have lead others to the RV rental experience.

Chapter 2, "Is It For Me?" offers advice, albeit sometimes a bit in cheek, to encourage you to step back and take an overview of yourself, your family and your objectives. The point of this chapter is to help you determine if an RV adventure is the sort of thing which would make sense for you.

Once you have decided on a rental RV vacation, it's time to get started on your next group of decisions. First turn to **Chapter 3, "Between Here & There"** for guidance on some preliminary planning issues. Then move into the critical materials in **Chapter 4, "Making Sense Out of Alphabet Soup"** (where you will begin the process of selecting your RV rental unit) and in **Chapter 5, "Choosing Your Rental Dealer"**.

PART 2 – DETAILS, DETAILS

In Part 2, you are guided through the maze of pre-trip planning and details. Here we tackle those things which are best handled in the days and weeks prior to your actual vacation.

Having selected, in **PART 1**, the area to which you are traveling, your dealer and your vehicle, it is time to turn your attention to the travel planning portion of the trip designing process. In **Chapter 6 – "Travel Planning"** we offer tips and guidance on the planning process. "Proper" planning – striking an appropriate balance between over-planning and under-planning – is a key step in crafting a successful RV vacation.

For many, the most intimidating part of an RV vacation is the RV itself. It is not only complex and involved, but it seems totally unfamiliar. You will learn that your "house on wheels" has pretty much the same systems as your "house of sticks and bricks". In **Chapter 7 – "What Is On Board?"** we introduce the basics of RV systems and equipment so you'll know what to expect.

Important enough to require a separate chapter, **Chapter 8 – "The Rental RV Kitchen"** opens with a discussion of the role the RV kitchen may – or may not – play in your RVing plans. We give you advance notice on what will, and won't, be in your RV kitchen and provide suggestions on equipping and stocking this important space. Here you will even find a few sample recipes to stimulate your culinary thinking.

Packing for an RV vacation is a different process from gathering things for an otherwise similar, but non-RV, trip. **Chapter 9 – "What Should We Bring?"** offers guidance in the packing (loading) process. With the help of the information in this chapter, and the checklists in the Appendix, you will be able to greatly reduce the chances of your forgetting something important.

PART 3 – LIFE ON THE ROAD

This section starts with **Chapter 10 – "Dealing with the Dealer – Part II"**. Here you will find out what to expect when you pick up your rental RV. We provide a "heads up" section covering things you'll want to watch out for and include specific questions for you to ask your dealer. Chapter 10 concludes by suggesting the first thing you should do as you head down the road in your new "home on wheels".

You have worked your way through the first ten chapters to get to this point. Finally you are on your way! **Chapter 11 – "Movin' on Down the Road"** and **Chapter 12 – "Campground Considerations"** deal with the day-to-day realities of living, and traveling, in an RV. Here you will find answers to the most common questions of those beginning their first RV adventure: "How do I actually live with and in an RV?" "How hard are they to drive?" "How do I set up in a campground?" and more.

Eventually, unless you decide to join over one million Americans who have made RV living their full-time lifestyle, you will come to at least a temporary end to your RV adventure. **Chapter 13 – "And Then We Were Done"**, prepares you for the process of returning your unit to the dealer and of returning yourself to the "real world". We include advice for those wanting to make RVing a more permanent part of their lives . . . and we suggest a mindset you can choose. A mindset where the adventure never really ends.

PART 4 – SPECIAL CONSIDERATIONS

Additional thoughts for the RV vacationer who decides on a fly/drive adventure are presented in **Chapter 14 – "Fly/Drive Rentals"**. In **Chapter 15 – "RVing With Pets"** we explain why a rental RV vacation need not necessarily exclude the family pet. Included are specific tips and advice on RVing with your pet.

Chapter 16 – "Other Special Circumstances" offers a few tips and some encouragement for those who would like to give an RV vacation a try, but have never pursued the possibility because of the special needs of a member of their traveling party.

MUCH MISCELLANEOUS & ESSENTIAL ETCETERA

At the back of this book are 40 additional pages of important information. Here you will find a glossary and a number of lists to entertain and educate. There are helpful forms and worksheets, seven valuable checklists, a section listing recommended books, and a list of helpful websites and mailing addresses.

LET'S GET STARTED

So, that's about enough ("More than enough", you say!) time spent telling you about what we're planning to tell you. Reading this book will place you on the threshold of an exciting new experience. Now it's time to sit back, pay attention and get ready for the open road!

WELCOME TO THE EXCITING WORLD OF RVING!!!

Part 1

Decisions, Decisions

Exotic Ideas
For Your RV Vacation

- *Drive to the Caribbean* - Rent an RV in Miami & Drive to the Florida Keys.

- *RV Down Under* - Rent an RV in Australia. Go it on your own or join an organized caravan.

- *Go Kiss the Blarney Stone* - Rent an RV in Dublin and tour the Emerald Isle.

- *Join a Caravan in South Africa* - Several Companies Offer Top Quality RV Caravans in South Africa.

- *How About Some Northern Exposure?* - Rent in Alaska or Canada and Drive to the Arctic Circle!

- *Do the Unusual South of the Border* - Take an RV for a Train Ride . . . or a Boat Ride . . . or Both. Join a "Piggy Back" Caravan to Mexico's Copper Canyon.

- *RV Under the Tuscan Sun* - Pick Up a Rental RV in Rome and Take a Leisurely Tour of Italy.

- *Visit Kiwi Country* - New Zealand is an Ideal Place to Tour in a Rental RV.

- *Travel to a Tropical Island* - Rent an RV on the Big Island of Hawaii.

- *RV the Viking Trail* - Check out New Brunswick, Prince Edward Island, Nova Scotia, Newfoundland and Labrador.

- *Bounce Down the Baja* - Join a Commercial Caravan and Drive All the Way to Cabo!!

- *Visit the Great Cities of Europe* - See "RV and Car Camping in Europe" by Mike & Terri Church.

- *Rent n' Rally* - Rent an RV and Join an Organized Rally. Go to Mardi Gras, the Pasadena Rose Parade, the Kentucky Derby, the Calgary Stampede - the Possibilities Seem Endless!! Check the Offerings by the Tour Companies Listed in Appendix D.

Chapter One
Why RV?

*T*hey seem to be everywhere; you can hardly miss seeing them – these houses on wheels. A part of you wonders about the people inside: What are they doing in there? Where are they going? And why have they chosen such a seemingly awkward means of travel?

The RV industry is stronger now than at any time in its history. RV ownership over the next 10 years is expected to grow more than three times as fast as the rate of growth in the general population. Who are all these RVers . . . and why do millions of apparently normal people buy self-contained homes on wheels? Let us first take a look at who these people are. Then, with that background, we'll dabble a bit with the question of why they travel by RV.

WHO ARE THESE PEOPLE WE CALL RVers?

About one out of ten vehicle-owning households in the US owns an RV. A total of 8.6 million households . . . and the number is expected to exceed 10.4 million by 2010. In terms of age, the largest group of RV owners, about 45% of the total, are between the ages of 35 and 54. Clearly a large portion, but from this we also know that more than half of all RVs are owned by people under the age of 35 or over the age of 54.

The average RV owner is 48, owns a home, is married, and has a household income of $47,000. Stated differently, the average RV owner is slightly older, marginally more educated and a bit more prosperous than their non-RVing counterparts. To this non-statistician, the differences are insignificant.

In fact, the conclusion one reaches – both from looking at statistics and from practical experience on the road – is that the "typical" RVer (whoever that is?) and the "typical" American (whoever that might be?) are the same person – at least on paper. So what is it that leads some to load up a bunch of stuff and take off to see the country while others are content to simply stay home? RVers are far too diverse to stereotype, but there are some generalizations we can be comfortable in making.

Stay At Home Types They Are Not – Starting with the most obvious, we can note that the RV community is not one of "stay-at-home" types. This is not a group of couch potatoes (perhaps lawn chair potatoes, but definitely not couch potatoes). As a group, these people we call RVers are more adventuresome, and more into curiosity, than their stay-at-home counterparts.

More Flexible/More Adaptable – There are many RVers who return to the same places year after year; however, there are a greater number using their RVs as bases from which to explore new places, see new things, experience new sights and meet new people. RVers are not particularly set in their ways. They tend to be flexible – to welcome the surprises, twists and turns which are inseparable parts of their chosen lifestyle.

WHY RENT AN RV?

For millions of families, **RVing means Freedom**. They find more convenience and greater comfort when they travel by RV. They are in more control than with other forms of travel. Everything wanted is right there with them. There is no need to drag suitcases in and out of the car – continuously packing and unpacking. They sleep in the same bed every night and can get their own meals and snacks anytime.

With around 450 national chain outlets and local rental dealers in the US, the rental RV segment may be the fastest growing portion of the RV industry. Many of today's RVers first tested the lifestyle as renters . . . and even those who own RVs have a lot of reasons for going the rental route.

There are few bad reasons for a first time RV experience; however, differing reasons do yield differing points of focus, differing goals and suggest differing approaches to the process. Let's take a look at some common reasons for renting an RV:

Our Friends Said We'd Love It – "Our good friends rented an RV for their vacation last year and had a wonderful time. We think we should give it a try this year."

A word of caution: If you have found you and your friends generally enjoy the same sorts of experiences, perhaps their enjoyment of their RV adventure is a good endorsement. Under those conditions, we'd say "go for it". On the other hand, don't allow your vacation to be simply a knee jerk response to the experiences of others. Don't allow others to do your vacation planning for you. Vacations are too short and too far apart to be spent marching to the beat of another's drum.

Wondering What It Might Be Like – A general curiosity brings many to the RV experience. It is something they have never done before. They find themselves wondering what it would be like, wondering if the lifestyle would suit them.

The only way to really discover what RV travel is all about is to try it. We have met many who, without ever having experienced it, are positive they would not like traveling by RV. Such people remind us of those who are positive they do not like, for example, Ethiopian food . . . without ever having tried it.

As mentioned above, curiosity is a common trait among RVers. If simple curiosity is a factor in your wanting to give RVing a try, know that you already possess one of the characteristics found in others who are enjoying the lifestyle.

Tired of Tenting – For many there is a progression in self-contained travel which goes something like this: backpacking leads to car camping leads to a folding trailer leads to a larger trailer or some form of drivable RV. Many of these "retired tenters" decide to try renting an RV because it feels like the next logical step, because they want to experience the outdoors in comfort. This group is highly likely to have a satisfactory RV rental experience. They already know that self-contained travel works for them and they bring a practical knowledge to the world of RV travel.

Renting Before Buying – Purchasing an RV is a major decision. One of the most common reasons for a rental RV experience is to allow for a sort of "extended test drive" before making the large, often frightening, commitment to purchase.

The renting before buying approach has much to recommend it. It gives potential RV owners a chance to try on the lifestyle before making a larger financial commitment. It gives them a "hands on" opportunity to find out which RV features are, and are not, important to their way of RVing. Many costly buying mistakes could have been avoided had the purchasers first rented an RV.

Widening Experiences – Many travel to see new places and to do things they've never done before. That they have never traveled by RV is reason enough to try it.

These are the same sorts of people who, drawing on an example from above, would eat in an Ethiopian restaurant simply because they have no idea what Ethiopian food tastes like. The purpose of the restaurant experience is to try something they've never tried before. The objective of the RV experience is to try something they've never done before. They may or may not like the food. They may or may not like RVing. In either case, they will come from the experience with a broader knowing. When the objective is simply to try something new, the likelihood of an unsatisfactory experience is almost nonexistent.

Widening Horizons – Want to visit Alaska, Hawaii, Mexico, Australia, New Zealand, Europe or South Africa? Why not travel in a rental RV? RVing is perhaps without equal as a manner of visiting foreign countries. Travel by RV and you become part of the community you are visiting. In most of the campgrounds in Europe, for example, you are likely to be the only North American.

In a similar vein, rental RVing is an outstanding way for Europeans to tour North America. It places them one-on-one with North Americans and provides an opportunity to not only see a place, but to know a people.

Single Purpose – Many rent RVs for relatively brief, single purpose outings. Examples include the obvious – taking the gang to a football game, rodeo, or car race – and purposes a bit less predictable – providing living space for house guests or a place to regroup during a marathon shopping day at the mall. Just about any situation where portable housing – with bathroom and air conditioning – could conceivably come in handy has been a situation served by rental RVs.

This book is more specifically targeted to the needs and questions of the generally longer term vacation rental; however, many of the tips, tricks and techniques contained herein are also applicable to the shorter term, single purpose user.

PERHAPS THERE ARE NO "BAD REASONS"?

There are few, if any, really bad reasons for a rental RV vacation. Any reason which gets the vacationer out on the road, traveling, living, experiencing life, is likely to be a good one.

$AVING$ TIP$

Don't Try to Keep Up With the Neighbors. Avoid allowing your RV vacation to become a sort of contest where the whole thing becomes about getting as big an RV as you can find and traveling as far and fast as you can. RV vacations are perhaps best experienced at a moderate pace and enjoyed in an RV scaled to your needs.

In the final analysis, the primary reason first timers rent RVs is to sample the lifestyle – to dip a toe in the RVing waters and to find out what this means of travel is really like. RV rental experiences at their best start with an open, curious mind and end with the participants knowing a great deal more than when they started.

You may decide to sell everything, buy an RV, and adopt a life of travel – in the US alone an estimated one million others are doing exactly that. At the other end of the spectrum, you may decide there is nothing about the RV experience worth repeating – the lifestyle doesn't suit everyone. You are likely to fall somewhere between these two extremes.

We can't tell you how you will be impacted by your first RV experience, but we can tell you how to find out – and that is the subject of the remainder of this book.

CAVEAT:
IT'S NOT NECESSARILY A MONEY SAVING DECISION

We have read that traveling by RV is as much as 70% cheaper than a traditional vacation. Such claims are irresponsible. They consistently include in the traditional vacation the cost of lodging, while in the RV vacation they ignore the cost of the RV. It seems the equivalent in logic to claiming a vacation at the Ritz is no more expensive than at Motel 6: true enough perhaps – *if* you ignore lodging costs.

Owning May Be Different – Admittedly if you own an RV, and ignore its cost, you can make a case for it being cheaper to vacation by RV than by any of the more traditional means. The logic here – we like to use this one ourselves – being that once you have an RV it is hardly more costly to use it than not. This part of the debate is meaningless to the potential RV renter. Your position is one of paying for lodging (renting an RV) or paying for lodging (staying someplace else).

Rough Cost Comparison – The costs of renting an RV vary depending on the size of the RV, the season and the region in which you are renting. The sorts of motor homes most commonly rented range generally from $90 to $200 per day (plus mileage and extras). Travel trailers are usually much less expensive to rent, but – for reasons we'll introduce in a moment – are not really an option for most of you. In addition to the cost of the RV rental, fuel costs will be higher than you are accustomed to.

You will also need to add in campground fees. While these can be as low as $10 or $12 (and can go up to well over $100) per night, you can safely expect sites in most commercial campgrounds to be in a range of $25 to $35. In high demand areas during peak season the average may be higher.

There are also savings – at least potentially – in RV travel. Entertainment costs are often lower (enjoying the RV and campground experience serves as a major source of entertainment). You also have the option of doing some, or all, of your own meal preparation – meals and drinks can cost about the same as if you'd stayed home.

When you add up the costs, subtract the savings and compare the answer to the expense of a more conventional vacation, you will probably find the RV a bit cheaper, but usually not by enough to serve as the primary reason for an RV vacation.

A LIFESTYLE DECISION

In the final analysis, a decision to try an RV rental vacation is best made from a place of curiosity and with a goal of seeking new experiences. Don't try to use economics to justify your conclusion – it may or may not work and is, in the final analysis, really pretty much beside the point.

Who should consider an RV rental vacation? Anyone who is attracted to the idea of the freedom of RVing, that's who: people who find appeal in the notion of going where they want, when they want and of doing so with all the comforts and conveniences of home. Perhaps people just like you.

With this background, we can now move into a more personal analysis.

Chapter Two
Is It For Me?

Prior to committing to an RV rental vacation, it is worth taking a bit of time to examine your objectives and the RV lifestyle with a goal of determining if they are compatible. Here we offer a few indicators, albeit sometimes a bit in cheek, which are intended to help you step back and take a look at yourself, your family and your objectives. The point is to determine, at least on a preliminary basis, if an RV Adventure is the sort of thing which would make sense for you.

DIFFERING OPINIONS, ONE HOUSEHOLD

Let's get this one out of the way first! In some households there will be less than total support for the idea of an RV vacation. We are neither marital nor family counselors and are specifically unqualified to mediate those differences. Here we can simply offer a few general comments:

First, as a general sort of statement, it is not a good idea to confine yourself in a small space (such as an RV) with someone who is there against their will. If differences of opinion exist, the time to reconcile them is before committing to an RV vacation. It would seldom be a good idea to surprise a reluctant partner or family member by showing up, unexpectedly, with an RV the day before your vacation starts.

Second, recognize there have been many, many cases where a reluctant, but open minded, partner has been pleasantly surprised by how enjoyable the process of traveling by RV can be. The key here being the notion of an "open mind". Anyone who enters into any venture, including an RV vacation, having already decided how agreeable they will find the experience, is likely to find an experience which pretty much matches their expectations.

Third, both those in the pro-RV camp and those on the other side of the question would be well served to remember that the future likely holds more than just this one vacation. A reasonable form of compromise might include an RV vacation one year and a non-RV vacation the next. Doing two differing types of vacation back-to-back offers a nearly perfect basis for comparison.

The key to a successful RV vacation (and remember that "successful" in this sense means simply that you have a good time and finish knowing more than when you started) is to approach the vacation with open mind and with joyful anticipation.

Finally, **recognize that not deciding is also a decision**. Unable to reach a mutually agreeable decision, many set the idea of an RV vacation aside. There is of course nothing wrong with that, just recognize that doing so is a decision – a decision *not* to take an RV vacation.

YOU MIGHT BE AN RVER IF . . .

Consider the Pros

There are perhaps as many reasons for traveling by RV as there are those who are doing so. Are there specific personality traits which assure a happy RV experience? NO, but there are some general indicators. Consider these:

You Might be an RVer If . . .

1. If you can't go to Wal-Mart without noticing the number of RVs in the parking lot, you might be an RVer.

2. If you like meeting people who have been places you've only dreamed of, you might be an RVer.

3. If you are convinced it is impossible to pack for an extended trip in two fifty pound suitcases, you might be an RVer.

4. If your idea of "all inclusive" is "Everything I need is around here somewhere", you might be an RVer.

5. If you love surprises, you might be an RVer.

6. If you would rather be outside watching a sunset than inside watching a floor show, you might be an RVer.

7. If you like doing things your way, you might be an RVer.

8. If you see an RV on the road and find yourself wondering about the people inside, where they are going and where they have been, you might be an RVer.

9. If you hate unpacking and then packing again every time you stop for the night, you might be an RVer.

10. If you like the idea of visiting new and exciting places, but also enjoy the comforts of home, you are almost certainly an RVer.

Summary of Positive Indicators

We hate generalizing. Not because we don't find it useful, but because we know that as soon as we attempt to sketch a simplified view of a highly diverse group we will hear from those who feel we have left out, or included, characteristics inappropriately.

Having said that, we will say this: As a group, RVers tend to be more active, more outdoor oriented, more adventuresome, more independent and better able to adjust to unanticipated occurrences than their non-RVing counterparts.

ON THE OTHER HAND, YOU MIGHT <u>NOT</u> BE AN RVER IF . . .

Consider Some Negative Indicators

Every reason favoring RV travel has its opposite. As mentioned in the previous chapter, about 10% of the vehicle owning households in the United States own RVs . . . which means that 90% don't. It could be there are far more people unsuited to the RV lifestyle than there are those who find it agreeable. So we reverse our question above, are there specific types of people who are simply not suited for the RV lifestyle? And again the answer is NO. And again there are some general indicators. Consider these:

You Might Not Be an RVer If . . .

1. If your idea of roughing it is when room service fails to answer on the first ring, you <u>might not</u> be an RVer.

2. If you feel nature is a thing to be directed and controlled, rather than observed and enjoyed, you <u>might not</u> be an RVer.

3. If spending your entire vacation in the heart of a big city sounds like perfection, you <u>might not</u> be an RVer.

4. If you <u>really like</u> dressing for dinner, you <u>might not</u> be an RVer.

5. If you hate making decisions while on vacation, you <u>might not</u> be an RVer.

6. If the thought of being separated from the TV brings feelings of anxiety, you <u>might not</u> be an RVer.

7. If you expect, when returning from an outing, to find your room has been cleaned and your beds made, you <u>might not</u> be an RVer.

8. If you think eating out-of-doors only benefits the ants, you <u>might not</u> be an RVer.

9. If you expect total predictability, you <u>might not</u> be an RVer.

10. If you don't know how to drive, you are <u>almost certainly not</u> an RVer.

Summary of Negatives

Those whose ideal vacation involves being pampered and catered to will find little papering or catering on an RV vacation. We are all for pampering, but we also recognize that, unless we make a decision to pamper and cater to one another, there is neither pamperer nor caterer included with our RV. Those who like structure and predictability on vacation will find that either is only present to the extent they decide to create it. Those who view a vacation as a time to simply shut down and leave all of the deciding and organizing to others will find the role of those "others" can only be filled by themselves. To paraphrase Pogo, "We have met the others and the others are us".

There is only one way to find out how well the RV lifestyle suits you. You could talk to one thousand friends, read one hundred books, take a dozen personality tests, but there is only one way to really know if the RV life is for you or if it isn't: rent an RV, load up some stuff, go someplace, have some fun. When you return you'll know a lot more than when you left . . . and that really is pretty much the point of the whole thing.

So, now what? OK, so you've decided to give the RV lifestyle a try . . . you may be a bit nervous about the whole process, but you're going to at least find out for yourself what it's like.

Now what? The next logical step, if you haven't already done so, is to decide where you are going on your RV adventure. We take a look at some things you should consider in Chapter 3.

Chapter Three

And Where is There?
(Between Here & There)

Here's The Thing . . . You could rent an RV, park it in your driveway and spend your vacation there. You could, and we suppose people have, but that sort of removes both the word "recreation" and the point of "vehicle" from the idea of vacationing in a recreational vehicle.

If we can start by agreeing that the central point of your rental RV vacation will be to travel someplace in a rental RV, then the first step in planning your RV rental vacation is deciding where that "someplace" might be. Then, having decided that, we need to work it out so that both you and your RV wind up wherever that is.

By definition, an RV vacation requires that – one way or another – you and your chosen RV wind up wherever it is you have selected. Just how you decide to go about accomplishing that influences both the logistics and the flavor of your vacation. The question is how to best bridge the distance between where you now are and where you intend to vacation.

Let's start by assuming you want to vacation someplace you're not and we'll note that it needn't necessarily be a place far away (though it could be). We will also guess that you already have a general idea where this place is that you want to go . . . and that it is a place somewhere beyond your driveway.

A good starting point is to decide if you want to rent your RV someplace near your home and drive it to your chosen vacation spot or if you want to travel first to your destination (either flying or driving) and rent an RV there.

$AVING$ TIP$

Plan to Fulfill Your Objectives. If, for example, your objective is to test out the RV lifestyle, then a destination close to home is worth considering. The further a field you travel the more costly the trip. Additionally, staying in or close to familiar territory will reduce outside complications and allow your party to better focus on the RV experience.

RENT AND DRIVE, DRIVE, DRIVE

The first, and for many the most obvious, option is to rent somewhere close to home and drive to your vacation spot. As with all options this one has, depending on where you now live and where you are intending to vacation, a range of pluses and minuses to consider:

Pros & Cons

Starting with an RV you've rented near your home has some important advantages:

First, consider the ease and affordability of loading/equipping an RV when it is parked in your driveway. For many, including the authors, a major benefit of an RV vacation is the ability to take a lot of stuff. More books than can be read, more clothes than can be worn, and a kitchen overly equipped. We will discuss the issue of "stuff" at length later in this book, but for now keep in mind that the simplest way of winding up with an RV full of stuff is to park it in your driveway and throw in piles of previously selected, presumably important, stuff.

Second, perhaps more than any other means of travel, traveling by drivable RV brings truth to the notion that "getting there is (more than) half the fun". Travel down the road with your passengers watching movies, playing games, or sitting comfortably watching the world go by. Cold drinks, snacks and a bathroom are all near at hand. Many of our most poignant memories of RV travel include images of us going down the road, heading towards new adventures and discoveries.

The question then is, "Why wouldn't we just automatically choose to rent an RV where we are and drive to where we want to be?" There is a one word answer: Distance. If your destination is "too far" from your point of beginning, the costs of a "rent and drive" vacation can become prohibitive.

$AVING$ TIP$

Less Driving Saves Money, but At What Cost? Your RV driving expense will probably be somewhere around 50 cents per mile (assuming a dealer mileage charge of 30 cents and an additional 20 cents for fuel). Reducing the number of miles driven can obviously produce significant savings. As an offset to those savings, keep in mind that traveling around in an RV is a big part – perhaps the single most important difference – of that which makes an RV vacation unique and fun. Be careful that you don't become so focused on cutting back on the miles driven that you end up cutting a sizeable portion of the joy from your vacation.

Driving down the road in your rental RV is certainly fun, but it isn't free. Your rental agreement may provide a minimal daily mileage allowance . . . or may simply assume you won't want to drive anywhere. Your cost per additional mile will be in the area of thirty cents . . . on a trip of a couple thousand miles those charges add up quickly. If the drive to where you want to be is one of a day or two or three, you will also have, in addition to mileage charges, extra days of rental fees <u>and</u> you will be eating up days of your presumably limited and precious vacation time.

You will also want to check rental rates both in the area of your home base and in the area of your destination. It is probable you will find noteworthy differences in rental charges in one area contrasted to another. In an extreme case, one where rates are significantly lower at your starting point than at your destination, it is possible to find cost savings in a rent locally and drive to destination sort of approach.

Other factors (specifically cost and availability) being equal, we would hesitate to use the rent here/drive there option on a trip of more than 300 or 400 miles (600 or 800 miles round trip).

DRIVE, DRIVE, DRIVE AND THEN RENT

Here the approach is that you load up your stuff and your traveling companions in some sort of vehicle (most likely the family car), drive to a metropolitan area near your planned vacation spot. There you rent your RV and continue on to your planned vacation spot. Again, consideration of this option requires understanding points favoring and opposing this way of doing things. The distances involved are admittedly a major factor, but the "drive there, then rent" option involves giving thought to things beyond the simple mathematics of distance.

Pros & Cons

This approach is best for what you might think of as "middle distance" destinations. There are those trips which seem too long to pay the extra use and mileage charges required by the "rent here, drive there" option and which also seem too short for flying to make sense. For a vacation involving such intermediate distances, take a look at this approach. Here are some factors to consider:

While not as handy as having an RV parked in front of the house, a lot of stuff can be hauled in the family car. The fact remains that having a quantity of your own stuff along on vacation blends the advantages of home with those of travel.

Given the daily and mileage fees involved in an RV rental, it may be cheaper to cover the distance in your existing vehicle rather than in a RV rental. Any way you travel from Point A to Point B involves some cost. For the majority of our readers, the notion of driving a reasonable distance in a vehicle already owned will be the least expensive option.

Arriving at the RV rental dealer's with your own vehicle does introduce one new twist which you should sort out in advance: What will you do with the family car while out charging around in your RV? Leaving it at the dealers may or may not be an acceptable alternative. How secure are the dealers facilities? Will the dealer allow you to leave your vehicle there? What alternatives does you dealer suggest? These are questions you need to deal with before finalizing your rental agreement.

Also, consider this: It might be in your best interest to caravan on your journey. Having brought your family vehicle this far, it might be worth while to bring it along on the remainder of your trip.

So, when a trip falls into that range of distance which is further than seems reasonable (as defined by you) to travel in your rental RV and yet short enough for driving to seem more practical than flying, this notion of simply driving to a place near your destination, and then renting, makes wonderful sense.

This option is one we would look at most seriously with destinations 400 to 1,200 miles from your home base. For shorter trips inject an additional element of fun – travel in the rental RV unit. For trips requiring several days driving time (and with reasonably priced flights available to a point near our destination), our suggestion is to preserve the vacation time and apply those funds you would have spent driving (fuel, lodging, meals and etc.) towards the cost of an airline ticket.

Consider a "Test Outing"

As an aside, we note the advisability of renting an RV locally, and for a short period of time, as a sort of "test outing". (Keep in mind that many RV Rental Dealers have minimum rental periods of a week during peak seasons. Many also allow shorter rental periods during their off seasons and shoulder seasons.)

A possibility we recommend is that of renting an RV locally in whatever part of the country you now live and going out to some place close to home for a long weekend. This test outing sort of beginning can be an ideal way of introducing the RV lifestyle.

Spend two or three nights in an RV and you will be, relative to what you now know, a seasoned veteran of RV travel. You will be amazed how much you can learn about selecting and outfitting an RV Rental Unit in a short period of time. You will be able to refine your understanding of RV living in an environment where there is little in the way of significant risk – you will be close to home and will not be gambling your entire vacation on your ability to anticipate correctly.

FLY THERE, THEN RENT

If you weren't doing an RV rental vacation, would you drive to your destination or would you fly? This core question leads us to consider the option of flying to the chosen destination and then renting an RV. Simply put, those vacation destinations to which you would, on a non-RV vacation, fly and then rent a car are also logical places to which to fly and then rent an RV.

That many of the larger rental companies offer fly and drive packages is an indication of the popularity of this type of RV rental vacation.

Pros & Cons

In this common approach to the RV rental vacation, the advantages and disadvantages are pretty straight forward. On the negative side are the increased costs and a number of logistical considerations. On the positive side are time savings and an ability to expand the number of places where it is possible to go on your RV rental vacation.

Assume, at least for now, that you can deal with the logistical issues. Millions of others have – that alone is probably evidence that you will be able to do so. In **Chapter 14** we will work with logistical issues which are specific to a fly and rent RV vacation. For now, we suggest you set those details aside and focus on some more basic considerations.

Start by looking only at the costs of the fly and rent option – consider both the extra costs in this approach and the cost savings. It is a fairly simple matter to calculate the dollar cost of driving from point A to Point B. Figure in mileage costs – fuel, maintenance, wear and tear – add meals and lodging and then subtract the resulting total from the cost of flying – including airport parking fees if applicable – and you'll have a good approximation of the net dollar cost of flying.

The cost of not flying is primarily a time cost. Take a look at the amount of time invested in driving from Point A to Point B. Look at flying as giving you the option of purchasing that extra vacation time for a predetermined fixed cost.

If you live in Florida, plan on an RVing vacation in Alaska and have 2 weeks of vacation time, then a "fly and rent" trip is the only reasonable option. At the other end of the scale, if you live in Denver and are planning a vacation in the Colorado Rockies it is obvious you would rent an RV close to home and drive it to your destination. Between those two extremes lie a series of judgment calls which only you can make.

$AVING$ TIP$

As you sort through various possible destinations, know that some are much more expensive than others. **Don't fall into the trap of selecting the most expensive of destinations** and then find disappointment in the high cost of your RV vacation.

CONSIDER <u>ALL</u> THE OPTIONS

Remain open to the seemingly infinite number of RV renting, driving, vacationing options. Be creative in your planning. Here are a few more ideas to further stimulate your thinking:

It is often possible to do a one-way rental where the RV is rented in one location and returned to another. (Some of the larger RV rental companies even offer special one-way incentives during the shoulder seasons as they reposition their rental fleets between summer and winter destinations).

Rental RVs are available in all 50 states – yes, including Hawaii. There are commercial RV caravans in Europe, Australia, New Zealand and South Africa. (These caravan packages include guides, campground fees, rental RVs and loads of extras.) Additionally, many RV rental dealers will allow you to take their units into Mexico – if you are traveling with an approved commercial caravan. In fact there are packages available for nearly any sort of RV rental vacation you can envision. Decide first what you would like to do on your vacation, and then start the process of figuring out how to make it happen!

You have made a few preliminary decisions. You have reached conclusions about where and when you plan to vacation and have an idea where you would like to take delivery of your rental RV. The next step is to decide what sort of an RV you'd like to rent. In the following chapter you will learn about the different kinds of RVs, you'll find out which sort of RV is the most commonly rented, and we will give you a bit of guidance to help you decide on the best type of RV for your first outing. Once you know what you want to rent, and where, we will (in **Chapter 5**) take a look at the process of dealer selection.

Chapter Four

Making Sense Out of Alphabet Soup

*I*n this and the following chapter we deal with the related issues of choosing your RV rental dealer and of selecting the rental unit best suited to your situation. We have divided what is in a sense one subject into two parts because that is what one does in a book such as this – divide a complex subject into manageable chunks of information.

As you move through this phase of your decision making process you are likely to find yourself moving back and forth between this chapter and **Chapter 5, Choosing Your Rental Dealer**. Your choice of a specific rental unit will be limited by the range of options available at your chosen dealer and your selection of a dealer should, in part at least, be based upon the availability of the sort of rental unit you are wanting.

Now that you are thinking about an RV vacation, you will notice more RVs on the road. It is likely you have an increased awareness of differences in RV sizes and shapes – of the huge diversity within this parade of things we call recreational vehicles.

Don't worry about it! While it is true there are a number of differing types of RVs, selecting your rental unit is not as complex as it seems.

TYPES OF RVs

The division of RVs into basic categories and various subdivisions is less complex than you might have assumed. In the following sections we review the sorts of RVs currently being manufactured and offer a bit of guidance to help you select the best option for your rental RV vacation.

There are two basic categories of RVs: those you tow and those you drive. (Just to keep things from getting too simple, there is also the Pickup or Truck Camper which you can neither tow nor drive – for these purposes we have included it in our discussion of drivables.) Here we cover these two basic groups, the subdivisions within each, and introduce some general comments about their suitability for your RV vacation.

TOWABLES

Based on the number of units sold, towables are the most popular general category of RVs. In this section you will take a look at what towables are, at the reasons for their popularity, and take a brief tour of the basic types of towables. You will also learn why it is <u>unlikely</u> you will select a towable for your first RV outing.

A caveat here: We currently own a 33 foot Fifth Wheel with 3 slides. Why do we own this unit instead of something else? Simply put, we selected this trailer because it suits us. We mention it here because we are entering into an area of known prejudice. We have had hundreds of marvelous days and an equal number of restful nights in our current trailer. With such an attachment it is difficult to be totally objective when looking at possibilities greatly different from ours.

What Are Towables - Generally?

Simply put, towables are RVs without motors. Because of the need to drag them from one place to another, they are generically called "travel trailers" or towables. These units have some significant advantages. A majority of RVers enter into RV ownership with one form or another of towable.

Advantages of Towables

There are some excellent reasons for the popularity of towables. It is worthwhile to take a moment to review them:

Cost. An entry level drivable RV costs around ten times what you could expect to pay for an entry level folding trailer. Cost is a major factor leading many to select a towable as their first recreational vehicle. In addition to the purchase of the trailer, the towable owner must also have an adequate vehicle with which to drag it around. A factor which helps make towables comparatively affordable is that most owners are also able to use their tow vehicle for daily transportation. For many, motive power for their RV does not require a totally separate vehicle.

$AVING$ TIP$

A Towable – typically a popup or travel trailer – is, for those with a suitable tow vehicle, a <u>far less expensive</u> rental option than any of the driveables. If you own, or have access to, an adequate tow vehicle, locating a rental dealer with towables in inventory can potentially cut your rental costs at least in half.

Space. A towable provides more living space, for less money, than a drivable. A drivable RV requires a "driving compartment" which generally isn't living space when stopped. This space requirement effectively shortens the drivable's living space by 8' or more. A 25 foot fifth wheel may actually have more living space than a 33 foot Class A motor home.

Servicing. Recently, while in Grand Lake, Colorado, we had a transmission problem with our tow vehicle. Getting needed repairs required that we leave it at a dealer's for more than a week. We rented a minivan, continued staying in our trailer and experienced little interruption in our travel plans.

A comparable mechanical problem with a drivable RV would have required that we put our entire house in the shop – creating an entirely different set of problems. Having your "motive power" separate from your "house" increases options and flexibility.

Tow Vehicle to Run Around In. A final plus comes when the RVer with a towable arrives at their destination, "spots" their trailer and disconnects. They then have their tow vehicle to run around in. A high percentage of those RVing in drivables tow a vehicle (called a "toad") behind their units for transportation when they have arrived at their destination; however, for reasons we'll cover in a moment, neither towables nor toads are reasonable options for most RV renters. They are only mentioned here to add to your general confusion.

TYPES OF TOWABLES

Towables vary in size, styles, amenities and costs. We offer here a brief run down of the basics not so much to aid you in your rental choice as to better equip you to understand what you are looking at as you roam the campgrounds in your future.

Folding Camper/Pop Up

Pop-up, Tent Trailer, Fold-Down Camping Trailer, Folding Camping Trailer – all differing names for the same sort of recreational vehicle. These are lightweight units which collapse, or fold down, for storage and towing. This type of unit combines the "next to nature" experience of tent camping with the weather protection, sleeping comfort and many of the basic conveniences of other RVs.

Although these units can cost $10,000 or more, their generally low price, coupled with their light weight and compact size, lead to their being a common entry point into the RV lifestyle for many. Once set up, these units include kitchen and dining areas, plus sleeping space for as many as 8 people. Options such as toilets, showers, stoves and refrigerators are available.

Travel Trailer

The **Travel Trailer** is the most popular of RVs. Depending on the size of the trailer, they can be towed behind cars, mini-vans, SUVs or Pickup Trucks. Larger models require heavy duty tow vehicles. Available in a large range of sizes and configurations, travel trailers provide the comforts of home for anything from weekend trips to full-time RVing.

There are also hybrid versions which combine a hard-sided trailer with pop-out ends which are similar to the fold-down trailers introduced above. Many travel trailers are available with "slide-outs" where a portion of the RV wall slides out to provide expanded living area. These units generally provide all of the conveniences of home in a compact, towable, "home-on-wheels".

Fifth Wheel

5th Wheel Trailers are designed to be towed by pickup and medium duty trucks equipped with special hitches. These are, from our admittedly biased perspective, the most residential "feeling" of all RVs. These trailers have bi-level sort of design with the bedroom, or living room, in a raised area over the truck bed. Many units present potentially spectacular views through large rear windows.

5th Wheel Trailers are available in a large range of sizes and cover the full spectrum of quality. The most spacious, largest and most elegantly furnished of fifth-wheels are wonderfully luxurious. Slide-out options are very common in this type of RV with some manufacturers offering models with as many as five slides. Because these RVs require a specialized tow vehicle they are seldom a practical option for the RV renter.

Park Models

Park Model Trailers are mentioned here because they exist, not because they are a reasonable option for the rental RV vacationer. These units are similar to large, conventional trailers, but are not designed with the idea of being moved frequently. In some areas, these units are available for rent in RV Parks and Campgrounds.

Think of these as functioning like a small cottage of less than 400 square feet and you'll have a good image of the lifestyle. Though renting such a unit offers a wonderful vacation option, their general lack of mobility places them outside of the coverage intended in this book.

WHY TOWABLES ARE SELDOM THE RENTER'S BEST OPTION

More space for less money, a vehicle to run around in when you get where you are going. It seems towables are an ideal choice for entering into the RV lifestyle – and if you were planning to purchase an RV that might be so. As a renter of RVs, towables are almost certainly <u>not your best choice</u>.

First, a towable requires that you have something to tow it with – a tow vehicle of some sort. And it is necessary the tow vehicle be set up for towing with special hitches and wiring and so on. Few first time RVers own suitable tow vehicles and of those with suitable vehicles an even smaller percentage are adequately equipped for towing RVs.

Second, pulling a large towable in a forward direction can challenge even the most experienced of drivers. Backing a towable, for those inexperienced in the backing of trailers, gives new meaning to the notion of "backwards" – the tow vehicle is turned to the left to send the rear end of the trailer to the right and visa versa. Newbies backing a towable for the first time are a popular form of campground entertainment.

Finally, if these reasons aren't enough to discourage the idea of a towable for first time RV renters, there is this: few RV rental dealers have towables in their rental inventory. So, even if you have a properly equipped tow vehicle, are comfortable backing trailers, and are convinced you would like to vacation in a rental towable, you may have difficulties finding a unit to rent.

DRIVABLES

Given that "towables" are RVs which you tow, it isn't hard to figure out that "drivables" are RVs you drive. The majority of RVs rented by vacationers fall into this category. Let's look at why that is.

Advantages & Disadvantages of Drivables

More Fun on the Road. Here is an area where the authors, that of course being us, must acknowledge the possibility of their work falling into the hands of a total idiot. By way of example, an article about stupid lawsuits which has been circulating for a couple of years relates the following story:

"This year's runaway winner was Mr. Merv Grazinski of Oklahoma City, Oklahoma.

Mr. Grazinski purchased a brand new Winnebago Motorhome. On his trip home from an OU football game, having driven onto the freeway, he set the cruise control at 70 mph and calmly left the driver's seat to go into the back and make himself a cup of coffee.

Not surprisingly the RV left the freeway, crashed and overturned. Mr.Grazinski sued Winnebago for not advising him in the owner's manual that he could not actually do this. The jury awarded him $1,750,000 plus a new Winnebago Motorhome.

The company actually changed their manuals on the basis of this suit just in case there were any other complete morons buying their recreational vehicles."

We don't know if this is a true story or not. The scary thing is that it <u>could be</u>. For that reason we want to be as clear as possible – **we are not recommending anyone, driver OR passenger, get up and walk around in a moving RV. We acknowledge that people could and do, we are simply saying it is a bad idea. Motor homes are equipped with seat belts and in most parts of the country it is not only a good idea to use them, it is the law. Remember all it takes is one sudden, unexpected maneuver to send unsecured passengers bouncing randomly around the RV.**

Having said that, we say this: One reason many choose an RV from the drivables category for their vacation is their superiority for trips which involving a lot of highway time (as contrasted to those involving extended stays in destination campgrounds). Traveling down the road while sitting at a table or on a sofa is a wonderful change from sitting full time in a conventional car seat. Cold drinks, snacks and bathrooms are all much more accessible than in their towable counterparts and, depending on the configuration of the unit, beds are often available for quick naps.

Less Space When Stopped. When compared to their towable counterparts, drivable RVs have smaller net living areas. A 30 foot drivable is 30 feet long bumper to bumper. After subtracting the portion of the vehicle allocated to the driver's compartment there is less living space than might be expected.

(A conventional travel trailer is measured from the front of the hitch to the rear bumper. In terms of living space, its length can be seen as overstated by the amount the hitch extends beyond the living area. To the extent a fifth-wheel's pin box extends beyond the front of the trailer, its length might also not accurately reflect available living space.)

$AVING$ TIP$

Think About Fuel Efficiency. Fuel efficiency is of course a relative thing. The notion of a fuel efficient RV may be the ultimate oxymoron. Having said that, some RVs do get better mileage than others. Other factors being equal (which of course they won't be) select the unit with the lowest projected fuel costs.

No Toads With Rentals. Many RV rental dealers do not allow you to tow anything behind their units – which would exclude towing any sort of vehicle. (It is also likely you currently do not own a vehicle suitable for use as a toad . . . and that makes the issue of dealer restrictions pretty much beside the point.)

TYPES OF DRIVABLES

Drivables vary even more widely than their towable counterparts in size, styles, amenities and costs. Prices vary from a few hundred dollars for a simple shell to place on the back of a pickup truck to well over $1,000,000! As a future RV renter, you are unlikely to find yourself at either extreme of the price scale. Here is an overview of the basic drivable RV categories:

Truck Camper

The **Truck or Pickup Camper** functions more as a drivable and so we have included it in this section. The fact is that it is actually neither towable nor drivable. These units feature a camper which is loaded onto, or attached to, the bed or chassis of a pickup truck. For our purposes the need for a suitable pickup truck eliminates them from consideration for the RV renter.

Pickup Campers range from nearly empty shells to large, fully equipped units. They are available in a wide range of floor plans and some even have slide-outs. Rarely are these available at the RV rental dealer's.

Class A

Mention recreational vehicles and the **Class A Motorhome** is the image which appears in the minds of many. These are the largest of the drivable RVs and often resemble buses. They are built on specially designed chassis and they can be found with every conceivable luxury. Prices range from under $100,000 to far over a million (we recently toured a unit priced at more than $1,500,000).

The less extravagant of these units are generally available at RV rental dealers. Some will be available with slide-outs and their rental costs are typically proportional to their size. Depending on the dealer, Class A Motorhomes are likely to be one of the two or three most available styles of RV rentals. Most experienced drivers will soon find themselves comfortable behind the wheel.

Pros & Cons

Class As are the largest, most impressive and most luxurious of drivable RVs. They are also generally the most expensive to buy and are correspondingly expensive to rent. For the first time RVer their size and the difference in perspective from the driver's seat can, at least for some, make them a bit intimidating to drive.

We recommend a "test drive" before you commit to renting a Class A for your first RVing experience. If you find the rental dealer's salesperson seems to be afraid to go with you on your test drive, consider that reluctance a thing worth thinking about.

Class B

The **Class B Motorhome**, also referred to as the **Camper Van**, is the smallest of the drivable RVs. The starting point for these units is a conventional van . . . and a great plus to the Class B is that it drives pretty much like a conventional van. Some feature raised roofs, some custom bodies, but they remain the easiest of the RVs to drive, many fit in regular parking spaces and they are comparatively easy on gas.

This improved maneuverability and improved fuel economy are not without tradeoffs. In the case of the Class B there are two: Being the smallest of the drivable RVs on the outside, it follows that they are the smallest on the inside. Too small for the tastes of some. Also, smaller does not necessarily mean cheaper. For reasons which are not clear to us, Class Bs typically cost more to buy than comparably equipped Class Cs . . . even more than the lower end Class As. This higher purchase price translates into higher rental costs. The rental RV vacationer may find the Class B option is a case of paying more for less.

Pros & Cons

Class Bs are the smallest of the drivables. This can, depending on your point of view, be either a major positive or a significant negative. Being basically a tall van, they drive like a tall van. Of all types of RVs, the Class Bs (and truck campers – an option we eliminated above) are the most "car like" to drive.

Class Bs have the smallest interior living space of the drivables. Some couples find the space adequate; others will feel claustrophobic. Those traveling with a number of children would be well advised to remember that deciding to live in one of these units for a vacation can feel like to spending two weeks shut up in the car with your children – day and night.

Before committing your vacation to a Class B – or to any RV as far as that goes – spend some time just hanging out in one either at an RV show or on the dealer's lot. You will never know specifically how well suited you are for a given type of RV until you have actually lived in it for an extended time, but hanging out in one for a bit can provide valuable insight.

Class C

$AVING$ TIP$

Renting a Class C or "Mini-Motorhome" – will provide you with more motorhome for less money than renting either a Class A or a Class B.

Class C Motorhomes (also known as "mini-motorhomes") are, with good reason, the most widely available of rental RVs. The most recognizable feature of the Class C is the distinctive cab-over bunk. Class Cs provide the conveniences of the larger Class As in a more compact, and lower priced, package. Given that the driver's area is actually a van cab, the perspective for the driver is not totally unfamiliar.

The Class C is the RV of choice for the majority of rental RV vacationers. They are typically equipped with the same living facilities as their larger

Class A cousins and they offer far more elbow room and storage than found in Class Bs. Depending on the size and configuration of the Class C, and upon the number in your traveling party, the cab-over area can be utilized as either an extra sleeping area or as additional storage.

Pros & Cons

Most RV rental fleets consist of no towables or truck campers, a few Class As, a few Class Bs and a whole lot of Class Cs. Most RV renters select a Class C and dealer inventories are simply a reflection of consumer preferences.

A Class C is neither as large and cumbersome to drive as a Class A nor is it as small and claustrophobic to live in as a Class B. Most find them to be an ideal sort of compromise which is both reasonably spacious and drivable.

As mentioned above, the driver's compartment in a Class C is a van cab. The perspective is not much different than in the driver's daily vehicle. In fact, the perspective can be too familiar – the driver must continually be remembering that the vehicle is significantly bigger than it seems from where she or he is sitting. It is taller, wider, longer and heavier – all factors to keep in mind as you drive about in your home on wheels.

REVIEWING THE OPTIONS

Towables – A Wonderful Option Which Probably Won't Work. If you already own a suitably equipped tow vehicle of adequate size and power and if you can find a dealer who rents towables and if you are OK with both highway driving and generally maneuvering a trailer, then a towable is arguably the best option for your first RV vacation. They are the least expensive to rent, offer the highest ratio of living space to vehicle length, and you will have your tow vehicle to drive around in at your destination.

Offsetting these advantages are the facts that towable rentals are more difficult to find than their drivable counterparts, you may not be comfortable driving and maneuvering a trailer, and few of our readers own a suitable tow vehicle.

Perhaps of greatest importance, it is simply a lot more fun to travel in a drivable RV . . . and having a good time is what vacations are all about. While we are personally aware of the positive aspects of towable RVs, we suggest the majority of our readers will find some form of a drivable RV to be best suited to their RV vacationing needs.

Drivables – Why They Are Your Best Option and a Caveat

Simply stated, within the two general categories of RVs – drivables and towables – nearly all of you will find your best option somewhere in the drivables group. There are two primary reasons this is so:

1st – No Tow Vehicle. First is that few reading these pages have, or have access to, an acceptable tow vehicle – one of sufficient size and power and which is properly equipped. Lacking an adequate tow vehicle, the elimination of towables from rental consideration is a given.

2nd – Availability. Even those with access to a tow vehicle, and with a desire to rent a trailer of some sort, are faced with an often insurmountable problem in locating acceptable, towable, rental RV units.

A Caveat – Lack of Toad. As previously mentioned many RV rental dealers will not allow you to tow anything behind their rental units. Additionally, you are not likely to own, or have access to, a satisfactory vehicle which is properly set up to function as a toad.

The lack of a smaller vehicle for running around is the sort of problem most of you can learn to live with. If you feel that may be too big of an inconvenience, consider renting a small car at your destination.

SELECTING YOUR HOME ON WHEELS

OK, so you've made, in a general sense, some decisions about the type of unit you want to rent. How do you now narrow the possibilities? Given the variety of options, how do you settle on one specific unit?

Most dealers do an outstanding job of guiding you in selecting the rental unit best suited to your vacation intentions. A few do an outstanding job of pouring you into the unit which they most want to see rented. It is good to have come to some conclusions on your own prior to approaching the rental dealer. Let's look at a series of considerations to narrow down to your options.

1st Consideration – Availability. First, given your preliminary range of selected possibilities, which units are available during your time frame and in the area where you want to take delivery? A bit of surfing on the internet, plus a few phone calls, and you can quickly come up with a list of realistic possibilities. There is no point in spending time planning a trip with a unit that simply isn't available.

2nd Consideration - Number in Party. Having determined available rental inventory in your target area, the next question is: How big of a unit do you want? And an important consideration within that question is: How many people will you be traveling with? As a starting point, it is probable most of the people in your party will want a place to sleep.

For those traveling with children, consider a fairly loose definition of "place to sleep". When traveling with small children, we have found they can be quite content, and feeling as if they are having a sort of adventure, with a sleeping bag on the floor. Older children can be most happy with a small tent for sleeping – it gives them a feeling of having their own space and, at least to some degree, gives them a bit of flexibility in terms of when they get up and go to bed.

The point here is that the smallest unit workable for your traveling group is the one in which you can make "acceptable" sleeping arrangements for all.

Notes on Special Factors

We conclude this book with a section of chapters dealing with special considerations. Here we present some factors you may need, or want, to consider.

If you have members of your party with special needs, be sure to address them early in the selection process. Does your group require a unit which has been pet free and/or smoke free? Conversely, do you plan to bring Fido and specifically need a unit where pets are allowed? Do you or members of your group have special needs in terms of accessibility? Most of these "special considerations" can be provided for, but since they are also factors which may serve to take a large number of units "off the table" they are issues which should be considered early in the selection process.

3rd Consideration – Cost. The larger the unit (within a given category) the more expensive it is to rent. These differences are often not as great as you might expect and, while it is a factor to be aware of, comparatively minor differences in size are seldom major cost factors when viewed in the context of the total cost of your trip.

An important aside here: The drivability of Class Bs makes them worthy of consideration – particularly for twosomes – as a first timer's RV rental of choice; however, they are both smaller and more expensive than the majority of Class Cs.

Perhaps the most important advice we can give here is to establish your price parameters in advance and then spend time looking only at those units which fit your budget. To do otherwise is not only pointless, but frustrating.

When you've reached this point in the selection process, you have determined the type of RV you are planning to rent – probably a Class C. You have, based on required sleeping arrangements, determined the smallest workable unit for your party and, based on cost factors, perhaps set an upper limit on the size of unit to be considered. Both of those areas are quantifiable and have served to narrow your choices. The next two areas of consideration are more judgment calls.

4th Consideration – Driving. First, at the upper end of the scale, come up with some guesstimation as to the largest sized unit you can feel comfortable driving. Not having had actual experience, this is a tough one. Until you actually get out on the road, about all you can do is give it your best guess.

Try to picture yourself not only driving down an Interstate Highway, but maneuvering in city traffic, driving on narrow mountain roads, and backing into a camping space. Don't get so vivid in this picturing that you decide to blow off the whole trip, but do give thought to size as a component of drivability. Generally speaking, additional length isn't as much an issue when driving on major highways. Length becomes more and more important as you attempt to maneuver in smaller and smaller spaces.

5th Consideration - Living Space. The question at this point in the selection process is one of "what is the smallest sized unit we can feel comfortable actually living in?" This is another important area in which you just have to accept that you can't really <u>know</u> with certainty until you have actually lived with an RV for a few days. You will find the space in an RV can shrink dramatically on rainy days (particularly when traveling with small children) and that the same space rapidly expands when the day is bright and sunny. Just give this one your best guess.

Think in terms of the smallest space in which you can vision being comfortable. You can always get a larger unit next time. And there is this to consider: if you find, for example, a 28 foot Class C to be unacceptably small, it is unlikely in the extreme you would find a 30 foot unit to be luxuriously spacious. Here again, you'll just have to go with your best guess, your gut feeling.

The "Sit Test". This is perhaps the most important, least quantifiable and final step in the selection process. Find a place where they have units much like those in the range you are considering – ideally the specific rental dealer you have selected. If your dealer of choice is part of a national chain, perhaps they have a local dealer with similar units. If the exact rental units you are considering aren't available, then go to an RV show or to an RV sales lot and find units as close to those you are considering as possible.

Pick a unit similar to the smallest you are considering. Sit in it and visit. Move around in it. Try both moving around in it at the same time . . . and accept that in all of the units under consideration simultaneous movement can be entertaining if not particularly efficient.

Now, select a unit similar to the largest unit you are considering and apply the same sit test. Does it seem significantly "better" (as defined by you)? Spend some time with it. Try to imagine what it would "feel like" to live in for an extended period.

After the sit test, you will probably have a good idea as to which feels better to you: small and cozy or larger and more spacious or perhaps a compromise somewhere in between? Just remember that only you know what seems best for you. Be careful about accepting the advice of salespeople or of well meaning friends.

> **TIP:** Take a camera along when you go to preview your future "home-on-wheels" . . . and take a lot of memory assisting pictures. Pay particular attention to getting a few shots of the kitchen area and of all storage areas.

FINAL RECONCILLIATION

Know that whatever your choice there will be things you will choose differently next time. A major reason for your RV vacation is simply to find out what it is like to live in and travel in an RV. That discovery process, by definition, will include much that is unexpected.

Your chosen RV will provide many pleasant surprises, but it isn't likely to be perfect. We have traveled in over a dozen RVs over the years. Our current 5th wheel seemed pretty much perfect when we purchased it. Now we recognize there are things we want to be different in our next unit.

You have now reached a point in your exploration process where you know more about the ideal rental unit for your RV vacation than anyone else. Go with that.

Having gone through the process of selecting a rental unit, you may very well have selected you rental dealer. It is after all a sort of chicken and egg type of deal. You can't reach final conclusions on one without having decided on the other.

There are on the order of 450 RV rental dealers in the United States – that is a lot to choose from! How do you, from this huge group of possibilities, go about the process of selecting the dealer which is the best match for you? As you have been thinking about the basics of your RV vacation, you have also done much, not all consciously, towards selecting your RV rental dealer. We'll take a detailed look at the process in the next chapter.

Chapter Five
Choosing Your Rental Dealer

*Y*ou have made some decisions about your RV vacation. You have reached at least some preliminary conclusions about what you want to rent (Drivable or Towable? Class A, B or C?) and where you want to rent it (Close to home, at your destination, in a larger metropolitan area close to your destination?). You have also, though perhaps not consciously, started the process of selecting your RV rental dealer. Of the 450 RV rental dealers in the US, you have eliminated all but a handful . . . OK, maybe two handfuls. The process of narrowing this group to a single, final selection can take a bit of time and may seem a little tedious, but you'll find it not particularly difficult.

LOCATION

The **First Step** in your process is to prepare a list of all of the dealers you can find in the general area where you plan to rent an RV. Search the Internet, the Yellow Pages, check with the local Chamber of Commerce. In this phase your objective is to come up with as many dealers as you can. Do anything you can think of to add names to your list.

> **Hint:** As you begin your search for an RV rental dealer, two good sources of dealer names are the **Recreational Vehicle Rental Association**: www.rvra.org, and the **RV Dealers Association**: www.rvda.org.
>
> (The **Recreational Vehicle Dealers Association** site will provide a list of RV dealers in your desired location. Not all of these RVDA members deal in rentals, but with a few quick phone calls, e-mails and a bit of study of their web sites you can pretty quickly figure out which ones do.)
>
> Both directories will give you phone numbers, e-mail addresses and, in most cases, web sites.

As you collect information, enter Dealer Name, Address, Phone Numbers, e-Mail and Web Site information on the "**Initial Possibles List**" found in Appendix B of this book. This part of the process sounds more time consuming than it is. It would be very unusual for you to find a huge number of dealers suitably located for your purposes. If needed, feel free to make additional copies of this work sheet for your own use.

When you are convinced your list of dealers is as complete as possible (or at least as complete as you are interested in making it) it is time to start looking for reasons to eliminate names from this directory of possibilities you have so carefully assembled.

RV TYPE, SIZE, MODEL

Step Two in your research is to review the decisions you made in Chapter 4 as to the sort of RV you are wanting. In this chapter you decided on your desired category of RV, most likely a Class C, on the size of unit which seems to work best for you, and perhaps even on a specific model. The next logical step is to eliminate those dealers which don't inventory units of the sort you are wanting.

Call, e-mail and/or check the dealer's web site. Use your "**Dealer Questionnaire**" and "**Dealer Comparison Worksheet**" (both also found in Appendix B) as a collection point for the information you gather from this point forward. When contacting the dealer be as specific as you can about the unit you are seeking. And, since methods of description can vary in the industry, be sure to describe what you are looking for and then ask, "Which unit or units in your inventory come closest to meeting my criteria?"

$AVING$ TIP$

Shop Specials. RV dealers often run specials – sometimes even in peak season. As you plan your RV vacation and work through the process of dealer selection be alert for specials being offered. Always ask, "If I can be flexible as to my dates of travel and/or the sort of unit I am looking for, do you have any interesting specials I should know about?"

Depending on how broad or narrowly defined your criteria, you may find you eliminate a number of dealers based on this single area of questioning. Place an "OK" in the column headed **"Inventory"** of each dealer which normally has a unit which seems like it would work for your purposes. NOTE: Dealers which have units which sound as if they are less than ideal, but which might still be acceptable, should not be eliminated at this point. Place an asterisk (*) in the Inventory column and make appropriate comments in the remarks section of the form.

AVAILABILITY

Step Three, continue down your questionnaire with only those dealers who pass the "Inventory" test. Ask about availability for the specific dates of your trip. If you have some date flexibility, be sure to share that information with the dealer's representative. Those dealers who have units such as you are seeking available during the time frame you have selected get an "OK" in the column headed **"Availability"**. NOTE: Dealers which have units available on less than ideal, but still acceptable, dates should also be left in the running for now. As you did under **Inventory**, place an asterisk (*) in the **Availability** column and make appropriate comments in the remarks section of the form.

"Jerk Factor"

As you move forward in your interviewing process you will find some of you talk with are lacking in people skills and/or come across poorly over the phone. Some may actually be rude. It's time to make your first judgment call. In the column headed **"Personality"** rate just how friendly and helpful you find the person on the phone. we use a scale of 1 to 5 with "1" being a total jerk and a "5" going to someone who at least is able to sound as if they have an interest in the success of our vacation.

What you do with this data is up to you, but we can tell you what we do with it. We are about to spend a significant, as defined by us, amount of time and money with the firm represented by the person on the phone. If that person can't manage to at least pretend to be concerned about our well being on this first, preliminary phone call, we assume they are unlikely to develop a deeper, more sincere interest in our welfare if problems arise during our trip. We draw a bold red line through the name of the firm and move on. This isn't very likely to happen, but your RV rental experience is too important to knowingly place in the hands of someone who simply doesn't care.

COSTS – Understand What You Are Getting

$AVING$ TIP$

Know What the "Base Rate" Includes. When comparing dealers, be sure you understand what each is, and isn't, including in the quoted base rate. You will find major differences in mileage allowances, included insurance coverage and in how the units are equipped. The cheapest base rate isn't always the least expensive.

Be sure you understand <u>exactly</u> what is included as "standard", what items are available as "extras" and precisely what the "extras" cost. Most rentals come with very, very little (as in nothing) in the way of non-attached equipment. As a rule of thumb you can assume anything which is not included as a part of the most stripped, basic RV imaginable is not included. In fact, a reasonable assumption is that the only inclusions are those things which are permanently attached.

I am not suggesting these things are always a significant point of competitive difference between RV rental dealers, though they may be. More I am suggesting this is an area in which you should be aware. Does your unit, for example, come with a microwave? A generator? These are items of importance. You might assume they are included – in many cases that would be an invalid assumption.

Most RV rental dealers do not include bedding, personal items, or cookware as part of their base fees. And most offer supplemental packages of these items (at additional cost). Just how significant these packages are in your specific situation depends generally on how well you are positioned to provide your own "stuff". If you are flying to some distant place to rent your RV, it probably isn't practical to carry cookware with you. (We note that it would be entertaining to watch you go through airport security with a carry-on full of pots and pans!)

At the time of this writing most RV dealers offer, as an option, some form or another of "Personal" kit. These kits generally include bedding, a pillow, a bath towel, dish towel and wash cloth. With some dealers the kit also includes an individual place setting of dishes and silverware. Costs for these kits vary depending on dealer and location, but you can expect to pay in the range of $30 to $40 per person as a one time charge for the duration of the rental period. These items are returned at the end of the trip.

Additionally, most dealers offer some form of a "kitchen", or "vehicle", kit. These include <u>very basic</u> kitchen and cleaning equipment. They are usually priced in the $75 to $100 range per vehicle and again this pricing is for the duration of the trip. These items are also to be returned (clean) at the end of the trip. Note here the words "<u>very basic</u>". Some do not even include fundamental survival equipment – such as coffee pots. Again, be sure you understand <u>exactly</u> what is included.

Other items – lawn chairs, car seats for infants, toaster – may be available at some dealers for an extra fee. Also, note that many rental units, perhaps I should say <u>most</u> rental units, are not equipped with a TV, VCR or any sort of stereo beyond that which is built into the dash. If these forms of entertainment are important parts of your vision of an RV vacation, you will need to make special arrangements. Ask the rental dealer for suggestions.

Make appropriate notes in the column on your form titled **"Inclusions"**. In the unlikely event you finish the dealer comparison process with two or more dealers ranked pretty much the same the information in this section can be used as a "tie breaker".

COSTS – Understand What You Are Paying

There are three basic fees, or groups of fees, in every RV rental. Dealers will have a variety of names for them. Think of them as a **use fee**, a **mileage fee** and a group of "**garbage fees**". As you enter into this area of cost comparison we advise you to first identify the use and mileage fees (and enter them in the appropriate area in the "**Cost Comparison Work Sheet**", found in Appendix B). Then dig as deeply as you can with the goal of uncovering <u>all</u> of the other fees applicable to your rental adventure.

Basic Fees: The basic, or use, fee is the daily, weekly or monthly fee quoted for the use of the unit and is usually pretty straight forward.

Mileage fees are more difficult to estimate and both the fee charged per mile and the daily mileage allowance, if any, included in your basic use fee can vary significantly. Be sure you understand exactly what the mileage fees are on each unit you are considering. With that understanding and a reasonably accurate estimate of the total miles you will be traveling, fill in the appropriate blanks on your Cost Comparison Worksheet. You will then have a good basis for mileage cost comparisons between dealers.

Other Charges: Be sure to ask each dealer, "What fees, taxes and/or surcharges will I be required to pay which aren't included in your quoted use fee?" If your unit is equipped with a generator (important if you plan to travel during the summer months, if you want to have electrical power available while you are traveling, or if you plan to camp where you have no electrical hookups) be sure you understand what fees are related to its use. Ask also, "what are your insurance requirements and/or recommendations?"

Each RV rental dealers will typically offer a variety of insurance options. Be sure to check with your insurance agent to see what coverage you have under policies you are already paying for. It is unlikely your existing policies will extend to your RV rental, but it is possible. Your agent can advise you on the pros and cons of the insurance options presented by the rental dealer.

Deposits: Find out what you will be asked to pay in the way of fuel, mileage, cleaning, dumping and/or pet (if applicable) deposits at the time of pick-up. Be sure you understand <u>exactly</u> what you must do to have those deposits returned to you at the end of your rental.

Finally: Ask, "Is there anything else I should, could, or have to pay to your firm . . . anything at all?" "Is there any cost – either optional or required – we haven't talked about?" Try to ask these final cost analysis questions as many ways as you can. At least 2 or 3 – more would be better.

Enter all these costs on your work sheet and arrive at totals for each dealer. Cost is clearly a factor of importance in your selection of an RV rental dealer. You are now in position to compare costs between those dealers appearing to meet your other criteria.

CLOSING COMMENTS ON COSTS:

First, be aware there are no miracles in the RV rental business. We urge caution if, without explanation, you find one dealer with costs significantly higher or lower than the others. We are not saying there are no legitimate reasons for cost variations. We are merely pointing out that you would be wise to view major variations as red flags indicating a need for further investigation.

Finally, we again acknowledge the importance of cost as a basis for comparison when sorting through a list of RV rental dealers. We also suggest it may not be the most important factor. If your unit breaks down and you then find your low cost dealer can't or won't provide service, cost will not have been the most important factor. If you arrive to pick up your unit and find there are none available, cost will not have been the most important factor. If you find your unit is filthy and/or poorly maintained, cost will not have been the most important factor.

We suggest you consider costs, even perhaps weigh them heavily. Also recognize that your objective is to have a memorable trip – an objective which is enhanced by selecting the dealer with the best reputation, best service, and highest standards of maintenance. If your only objective is to save a few bucks, you might be better served to simply stay at home.

$AVINGS TIP$

Travel in "Shoulder Seasons". Rental usage fees vary significantly depending on the time of year you decide to travel. Most dealers divide their year into "Peak Seasons" (the time of highest demand and of highest rates – and largest crowds), "Shoulder Seasons" (moderate demand and rates) and "Off Season" (lowest demand and rates).

Unless you specifically must travel during peak season, consider a trip during the shoulder seasons. Depending on the part of the country, you will frequently find outstanding weather, smaller crowds and lower rates (typically 20% to 40% lower) for a trip during these times. Conversely, trying to travel by RV during the generally unfavorable weather of off seasons is typically more trouble than the cost savings are worth.

LOCAL OR ONE-WAY?

OK, just a few more issues to touch on and then you will be ready to make your final dealer selection. An aspect of RV renting which can potentially limit your dealer selection is the idea of one way rentals – renting your unit in one place and returning it to another.

Advantages of One Way Rentals. One way rentals can add another dimension to your vacation possibilities. Rather than being limited to "out and back" or circular routing, one way rentals can enable you to plan linear journeys.

As an example, say you'd like to explore a big section of the west coast. With one way rentals you could pick up your rental unit in perhaps Portland, OR, amble down the coast at a leisurely pace, and return the unit in the San Francisco area. By structuring things in this manner, you save having to drive all the way back up to Portland. You save on the order of 10 or 12 hours driving time. You save around 650 miles worth of mileage charges. With the time you save, you can go further than you might otherwise have done . . . or you can cover the same amount of distance at a more leisurely pace.

Disadvantages of One Way Rentals. There is a price for the convenience of a one way rental. The fee for driving from Point A to Point B and not returning to Point A is called a "drop charge". Drop charges vary, but are commonly in the $500 range – a hefty fee partially offset by a savings in mileage charges.

Airfares vary widely and fluctuate constantly, but it is worth noting that two one way fares (flying to Portland and back from San Francisco in our example) are likely to be more costly than a round trip to either destination.

A one way rental has the potential to greatly expand your travel possibilities. This added flexibility, when it otherwise complements your plans, can be more than worth the extra costs and inconveniences.

$AVING$ TIP$

Extra Costs of One-Way Rentals. A one-way rental can dramatically expand your vacation options . . . and your costs. Rental dealers typically apply a "drop charge" of around $500 to one-way rentals. Additionally, buying two one-way airline tickets is frequently more expensive than a single round trip ticket. Give careful consideration to costs before committing to an RV rental vacation which includes a one-way rental.

Limited Dealer Selection. So, why are we talking about one way rentals in a section on dealer selection? Simply put, not all dealers offer a one way option. If a one way rental is your objective, you probably will have to limit your dealer selection to those with facilities in both your city of origin and your destination – and within that group you may find some who do not offer one way rentals between your points of choice.

CHAIN OR INDEPENDENT?

A final consideration, do you deal with a local independent (or perhaps even directly with an owner) or do you go with one of the big chains? As is true of so much about this process of selecting your RV rental dealer, the issue here is one of trade offs.

Big Chains

As you have probably found from your research to this point, a significant portion of your RV rental options involve multi-dealer organizations in one form or another. If you are not renting locally, these larger organizations often will be your best option.

Advantages: To our thinking, one of the single largest advantages to the big chains is that you can often view locally units identical – or at least very similar – to units you are intending to rent in a distant location. You can see how well the floor plan and size of the unit "fits", you can see first hand the level of cleanliness and make some judgments about maintenance standards (though these can vary from outlet to outlet within a given organization). In short, dealing with one of these organizations can give you a "hands on" sort of experience in the rental selection process which would hardly be convenient if dealing with a small independent in a distant location.

Big chains are positioned to offer economies of scale often unavailable through smaller operations. They frequently offer a wider range of rental options, better off season specials, more inclusive options for outfitting your rental unit, and are often better positioned to provide for the RVer with special needs. They often use their size to negotiate better roadside assistance programs.

If you are considering a one way rental sort of vacation, these can be difficult, often impossible, to arrange through dealers not affiliated with some sort of multi-outlet organization.

There are of course other advantages to dealing with the larger outfits in your search for an RV rental dealer. Some will occur to you and, if you just ask, the dealer's representative will be more than happy to share others you may not have thought of. Ask "Why would I be better off dealing with your firm than one of your competitors?" In response you will likely get a standard sales pitch – within it you may find advantages unique to the specific dealer and which strike a cord with you.

Disadvantages: In some cases inflexibility goes hand-in-hand with size. With these companies, size may mean they have an inflexible system which does a pretty good job of providing rather generic units, under a standardized set of terms, to the average renter. To the extent your ideals differ from those of the "average" renter, you may find a degree of inflexibility which makes the large dealer perhaps less able to design a rental proposal suited to your objectives.

Local Independents

There are a lot of local independents, but they can be harder to locate than the big chains with their massive promotional budgets. You may find these independents are worth the extra effort required to find them.

Advantages: Depending on your specific needs, there are a number of reasons why dealing with a local rental source – one not a branch of one of the larger chains – can be to your advantage. Here are a few to think about:

The further your criteria for type of unit, desired rental terms, and sought after inclusions differ from the statistical norm, the more likely you are to feel like a square peg being shoved into a round hole as you attempt to arrange a rental through one of the larger, more structured outfits. You may find an independent better able to adjust their policies to your specific needs.

Many who rent RVs do so to get a feel for the life style before buying. If this describes you, and particularly if you've looked enough as a potential buyer to have a good feel for what you plan to purchase if it all works out, then keep this in mind: many RV dealers who sell units also have rental programs. And many of those programs will give you a credit for at least a portion of your rental costs in the event you decide to purchase.

There are local rental dealers who act as agents for owners of RV units who are covering a portion of their ownership costs by renting their unit out for part of the season. In the event you have access to such a dealer, or middle man, know that these units often have far more bells and whistles (are far better equipped) than their more Spartan brothers in the rental fleets.

There are other positives in dealing with the independents. Some will occur to you; however, the easiest way to assure you don't overlook any is to ask the dealer why you should rent from them. As we suggested above when talking about the large chains, give the independent an opportunity to make their own case.

Disadvantages: The disadvantages in using a local independent are generally the flip side of the Big Chain's advantages . . . and visa versa. As you think about it, these disadvantages will largely be self-evident. Your best

---

$AVING$ TIP$

Take Advantage of Advance Purchase Discounts. Some RV Rental Dealers will offer discounts for early bookings and for early remittance of payments. Watch for these opportunities and take advantage of them when it makes sense for you to do so. **CAUTION:** Before prepaying, find out what refund policies are in the event you need to cancel your trip.

---

source of information in this arena is to simply ask a representative from one of the bigger chains. Don't phrase your question specifically to target a given independent, stay general. Ask, and then be quiet and listen.

Convenience vs. Economy vs. Dependability

It seems like there are so many factors to consider before committing to a specific dealer, to a particular RV rental unit . . . and there are. In your analysis, you may have found one dealer who clearly stands out as superior in all areas of importance to you. One dealer who is most convenient, whose costs are the lowest, who has exactly the sort of unit you are looking for available at exactly the time you need it. You may have found such a dealer and, if so, consider yourself fortunate.

In the End It's a Balancing Act. And for those who have not found such a dealer? Dealer A has the nicest units, Dealer B the best prices, Dealer C is ideally located and perhaps a fourth dealer has the best reputation of all. How do you reconcile all of that?

Recognize that, to an extent at least, you are comparing apples and oranges. And it is here personal preference must enter into your selection process. Only you can decide which factors are the most important in terms of your vacation.

In our family, for example, cost – within reason – isn't typically the number one factor. The point is to have a nice vacation. If saving money were the primary objective, we would stay home. On the other hand, cost variances can be so significant as to make the difference between going and not going.

That is significant. If cost differences are large enough to impact all other aspects of the trip, then cost is a factor to be considered. Perhaps your option is to rent Unit A and travel in style . . . and also be unable to eat for two weeks. Or, you can rent Unit B, be a bit less upscale, and have plenty of spending money for the remainder of the trip. Cost can be significant, but usually the differences you find will not be large enough to have a major impact. Our point is to recognize the importance of cost, but not to allow yourself to get so hung up on the saving of a few dollars that you make decisions which adversely impact your entire vacation.

For most reading this, the single most significant factor is the actual rental unit – its quality, condition, and general suitability for your traveling party. Keep your eye on your goal – to test out the RV lifestyle and to have a good time doing so – and your choices will become more obvious.

Perfection Probably Isn't There. For most, the absolute perfect situation won't be found. Accept that. Compromise on those areas you view as being least important.

Review Your Worksheets

"Cost Comparison Worksheet". As you consolidate your research, return to your "Cost Comparison Work Sheet". Review the information gathered to be sure you have not left anything out and that you are confident your estimated totals are at least in the ballpark. Look over those totals. Are any so high or so low as to tip the scales of judgment to favor or eliminate a specific dealer?

"Dealer Comparison Worksheet". The point of this work sheet has been to narrow the number of dealers under consideration in your selection process. For some of you, the process of working through the "Dealer Comparison Work Sheet" will lead to the conclusion there is only one dealer positioned to provide the sort of unit you have selected, at the time you want it, and with the ability to orchestrate the process in a way that works for you.

Others will find the process has turned up 2 or 3 possibilities – it is not likely there will be more than that. Presumably you will find you have not rated all dealers as equal in all areas. Look to the dealer which seems best in the areas most important to you. That a dealer offers an option for a well equipped kitchen is obviously of no advantage to those approaching their RV vacation with no intention of cooking. The dealer which is a few dollars cheaper, but has units you judge inferior holds no advantage.

Only You Can Decide. <u>Now it's decision time</u>. You have gathered far more information and know significantly more about your options than does the average RV renter. In fact, if you have done your homework, you are now in a place where no one knows more about the RV rental industry – as it applies to the vacation your family intends to have – than you do! <u>Make a decision</u>, review the paperwork thoroughly and get that most ideal of options tied up before someone else does!

$AVING$ TIP$

Does Dealer Offer Repeat Customer Discounts? Some rental dealers encourage customer loyalty by offering discounts to returning customers. Ask your dealer before booking your reservation. It may seem a small point now; however, it could mean a significant savings if you decide to continue your RV rental adventure beyond the first trip.

Oh Good, Paperwork!

OK! OK!! The paperwork is an important part of the RV rental process. And you ask, "if it's so important, why is it mentioned last". An excellent question:

First, as would perhaps be expected, the paperwork, in terms of who has and does not have which rights, is heavily slanted in the dealer's favor. While we, like you, may not like it, that's just the way it is and, generally speaking, like it or not, the paperwork is not negotiable. It favors the dealer because the dealer has by far the greatest stake in the transaction – an asset valued at tens of thousands of dollars. It is in their interest to protect themselves and that asset.

Having said that, it is still important for you to read and understand the paperwork. Ask the dealer <u>in advance</u> for copies of <u>everything</u>, read it all, get any questions answered. Finish your paperwork review <u>before</u> you show up to take possession of your unit. If you find something in the paperwork which is just totally unacceptable (you will), ask all other dealers you are considering for copies of their paperwork and compare to see if there are significant differences (not a likely possibility). Then, with an in-depth understanding of the rights you won't have, grumble a bit. Ask to negotiate the worst of the clauses (not likely to happen, but it doesn't hurt to ask). And then be prepared to sign away your rights at the time you take delivery of your unit.

Finally, we're done with the preliminaries. You've selected a destination, a rental unit, and a dealer. The basics are now in place. The process to this point has been a bit tiresome and, for many of us, not a great deal of fun.

Next we move into another preplanning arena. This one we suppose will also seem a bit tedious to some, but is an area many enjoy: We will now start filling in some of the details on your plan for a rental RV vacation.

Part 2

Details,
Details

Common Mistakes
of RV Renters

- Planning to do too much.

- Driving too fast or too long.

- Forgetting their unit is wider, longer, _taller_ and _heavier_ than the vehicle they are used to driving.

- Driving into areas, such as parking lots, without first planning how to drive out.

- Assuming their rental unit will have a TV, VCR, and/or Entertainment Center.

- Assuming their unit will be delivered with all of the equipment and supplies needed to actually live in it.

- Not allowing enough time for just enjoying the RV lifestyle.

- Planning to eat _all_ of their meals out . . . or planning to prepare _all_ of their own meals.

- Rushing through the dealer's pre-delivery orientation.

- Not paying attention to their monitor panel.

- Driving with the water heater or water pump on.

- Failure to Use Checklists.

- Hesitating to ask questions of other RVers.

Chapter Six
Travel Planning

Vacations begin before they ever actually start – there is heightened anticipation and an increase in eagerness as the RVer steps into the planning process. The vacation becomes more tangible as plans are fleshed out, new layers of detail penciled in. The planning process is more than simply developing a scheduling roadmap for a physical journey. It is the process which builds the mental bridge between where you now are in time and the actual day you depart.

$AVING$ TIP$

Planning Helps Avoid Impulse Decisions. Starting out with at least a general, outline sort of itinerary will provide a framework within which you can evaluate new vacation opportunities as they come along. Those things you decide to do on the spur of the moment can be the icing on the cake of your vacation experience. To the extent such impulse decisions take you outside your intended budgetary framework, they can also be expected to increase your vacation costs beyond what you had originally planned. We encourage spontaneity. Here we are suggesting you be aware of its costs.

THE ROLE OF PLANNING

Vacations have this in common – the traveler leaves home, goes some place, does some stuff and returns. Vacations usually start with a predetermined beginning and a known end. The point, it seems to us, is to create some pleasant memories in the times between. If you can manage to do some interesting things, preferably with a bit of style and a touch of eccentricity, then it is likely you will return feeling satisfied with your experience. Inherent in the travel planning process is the fact that events which actually occur on your vacation will differ from the events you plan. We encourage you not to think of your planning as a process of developing a rigid, precise, minute-by-minute forecast of future events. Travel planning, at its best, serves to create a framework within which decisions can be made as additional information becomes available.

Travel, at least in part, is a search for the unknown and unexpected. Self-contained, self-guided, self-structured travel – specifically travel by rental RV – will tend to increase your encounters with both the unknown and the unexpected. Your goal as a travel planner is to set aside slots of time for those things you want to be sure are included while leaving time open for spur-of-the-moment pleasures.

Concerns About Under planning

One of the advantages of the RV lifestyle is the increased flexibility compared to other types of vacations. You can, depending on the time of year and part of the country, get away with very little advance planning. You can be a bit of a free spirit drifting with the tides, deciding on things as you go.

Some of our most memorable RV trips have been those long weekends where we start planning at the bottom of our driveway. Do we turn left or turn right? These unstructured trips have been memorable, but not particularly efficient. We understand when we turn left we eliminate all we might have seen and done had we turned right . . . and in our situation that is OK. When traveling close to home, there is always the option of making a different decision the next weekend.

For a more standard vacation (presuming "standard" includes more distant destinations), we step up our level of planning. The key is to plan enough to ensure the inclusion of those experiences which are viewed as really important and to do so without becoming so regimented we loose the sense of freedom which attracted us to the RV lifestyle in the first place. The risk in under planning – in taking a sort of "go with the flow" approach to any trip and scheduling nothing – is that scheduling nothing pretty much guarantees that nothing is what will get done. "I woke up in the morning with absolutely nothing to do and went to bed that evening having only accomplished about half of it."

Dangers of Over planning

At the other end of the vacation planning continuum is the severely over planned vacation. The type of thing where you allow one hour to visit Mt Rushmore and stick with that schedule regardless of what you find when you get there. You must accept the risk your party may wind up leaving Mt Rushmore without having really seen it . . . not really perhaps knowing much about it. It can be seen as a sort of "trophy traveling" – checking a series of predetermined objectives off of the "been there/done that" list without ever really having experienced any of them.

Most vacations, RV travels included, start with at least a minimal level of structure – predetermined beginning and ending points. The danger is in so totally scheduling the time between as to leave no opportunity for the spontaneous.

$AVING$ TIP$

Don't Over Schedule. Scheduling too much into your limited vacation time often leads to a sort of frantic scurrying around as the vacationer attempts to do, and pay for, more than can be enjoyed in the limited time available. Far better in our judgment to try to do less, enjoy the journey more, and save a few bucks.

Each traveling group needs to find an acceptable balance between under planning and over planning.

Event Planning

The "things to do" portion of the planning process isn't greatly different for the RVer than for those traveling by auto and motel. You simply decide what it is you want to do and set aside time for the doing. We encourage you, in you planning, to incorporate the freedoms inherent in the RV life style by attempting to "error" on the side of under planning. Consider planning for those experiences you consider most central to your travel purpose while leaving open as much time for unanticipated pleasures as possible.

$AVING$ TIP$

Contact the Visitor Center and/or Chamber of Commerce In Each Area You Plan to Visit. You can find their numbers on the internet or through directory assistance. Tell them when you plan to be in their area and ask their advice on places to go and things to do. Most will be able to send you maps and brochures. Many will even have local newsletters where you can find lists of events scheduled during the time of your vacation. Take a few minutes to visit with these representatives; they can probably even suggest a few things outside of the normal tourist routines which could be ideal for your family.

Plan Around "Centerpieces" – a centerpiece being the single most important thing to see or do in a given segment of time. The point of planning in this way is simply to insure time for these most important experiences. The process starts with a question: "What is the single most significant thing we want to do this week (or this day or this afternoon)?" Consider a planning approach where you "schedule" these most important experiences fairly rigidly and then to allow the rest of your schedule to sort of randomly flow around your centerpieces. By way of example: the single most important thing about a two week trip to Florida might be a trip to Disneyland. The single most important part of a day in Key West might be Mallory Square for sunset. A trip to Northern California might have as its centerpiece a day in the Napa Valley. A day in the Napa Valley might be built around a visit to a specific winery and so on and so on.

$AVING$ TIP$

Consider a National Parks Pass. If your vacation plans include visiting several of our National Parks, a **National Parks Pass** is a potential money saver. It is an annual pass that provides admission to any national park charging an entrance fee. At the time to this writing, the pass costs $50 and is valid for one full year from first use in a park.

The point is that trips are best built around those focal points, or centerpieces, which add the greatest meaning and the most spectacular memories to your travel experience. Note also that your focal points don't have to be about <u>doing</u> anything. We have frequently found ourselves in an exceptionally nice campground or even in an outstanding site in a fairly ordinary campground and concluded the highest and best use of our time would be to schedule a "do nothing day" . . . one where we could just hang out and enjoy our surroundings.

We suggest you begin your trip planning by penciling in, scheduling, your single most important event. If there was only one thing you could do on this vacation, what would it be? Answer that question and then schedule it. (If your "centerpiece" is an out-of-doors activity, try to leave flexibility in your schedule so that you can reschedule this most important of events if the weather doesn't cooperate.) Then move down your personal hierarchy of importance until you have reached an appropriate level of planning – as defined of course by you. In the **"Scheduling"** section of our publication **"Trip Planning for RV Renters"** (available at www.RVRentalGuide.com) we have included sufficient time slots to allow the scheduling of every waking moment. We recommend you don't do that.

As mentioned, the event/activity planning process of the RV traveler doesn't really differ much from the planning of the non-RV traveler. There are two areas which *are* different: driving time requirements and campground selection. Here we touch on each area as it relates to the planning process. More information is found in **Chapter 11 – "Movin' on Down the Road"** and **Chapter 12 – "Campground Considerations";** however, the following is specific to the planning process:

DRIVE TIME CONSIDERATIONS FOR THE RV TRAVELER

Simply stated, you are best served by not planning to travel as fast, as long, or as far as in your rental RV as you have perhaps come to consider the norm in a more conventional vehicle.

You "Shouldn't" Go As Fast. RV travel is best when not viewed as some sort of race.

In your trip planning, keep in mind that it isn't wise to drive as fast in your RV as you might in the family car – though we acknowledge that you could. Your RV is taller, wider, longer and, of perhaps most importance, considerably heavier than any vehicle you are likely to be familiar with driving.

This is not to say your RV will be "difficult" to drive. It is to say it will be "different". Its extra size requires you to simultaneously keep your attention on things close to your RV and on events much further ahead than you may be accustomed to considering. Keep in mind that virtually everything you will want to do when driving your RV will take longer than in the family car – accelerating, passing, changing lanes, <u>and stopping</u>.

Factor these differences into your RV driving. We suggest you drive slower than you otherwise would in a given set of circumstances. (Your gas mileage will also be much better at lower speeds.) If this means driving slower than the normal flow of traffic, don't worry about it. When lacking passing lanes just remember to pull over periodically to let following cars get around you.

You "Shouldn't" Go As Long. RV travel is best when not viewed as an endurance contest.

The differences in RV driving require greater focus, greater attention and for most mean that driving a given time can be more tiring in an RV than driving a similar amount of time in a more familiar vehicle. The point of your vacation should be something more than exhausting yourself charging around from one point of interest to another. For planning purposes assume that not only will you be driving slower than you might normally drive but that you will also be driving fewer hours at a stretch. For many this adjustment won't need to make a planning difference. For some it will. Our point simply is that your trip will be more enjoyable in the absence of marathon driving days.

$AVING$ TIP$

It is seldom a good move to join the Good Sam Club or to get a KOA Value Kard with the intention of saving money on a one week trip. A **KOA Value Kard** costs $14 and will save you 10% off of the daily rate for stays at **KOA**. (Exception: If the card is purchased at a KOA Kampground, the maximum savings benefit for the stay in which the card is purchased is $14.) A **Good Sam Club Membership** costs $19.00 and saves you 10% at the network of more than 1,700 **Good Sam Parks.** In either case, it is unlikely you will use the card enough on a one week trip to recover your cost. Take a look at your campground plans before deciding. At best you can expect it to be a marginal investment.

CAMPGROUND CONSIDERATIONS OF THE RV TRAVELER

An important part of the preplanning process is the selection of campgrounds. A key to the success of your trip may prove to be the consistency with which you find your self stopping – be it for a week, a few days, or a single night – in campgrounds you find pleasing. Selecting pleasantly acceptable campgrounds isn't difficult; however, trying to wind up consistently in the best spot in the best campground can require a lot of research and planning far in advance.

Types of Campgrounds: There are two general categories of campgrounds – public and private. "Private campground", as the term is generally used, refers to those campgrounds which are privately owned. "Public campgrounds" are operated by a governmental entity of some sort.

Public Campgrounds – What You Should Know. The public campgrounds most likely to factor into your trip planning are federal campgrounds (National Park, National Forest and BLM) and those of the various state park systems. In some areas, you will find nice county or city operated facilities. The county and city campgrounds are generally more difficult to research.

Simply put, there are a lot of gems, in the various public campground systems. Compared to the private campgrounds, these tend to be more scenic, further off of the beaten path, and better situated for your enjoyment of the area's natural wonders.

It is also true these campgrounds are frequently not able to accommodate even moderate sized RVs, they are often lacking basic hookups, many have only pit toilets and few have shower or laundry facilities. Getting reservations in the best of these campgrounds requires knowledge, planning as far as a year in advance and often a bit of luck.

Our personal routine is to stay in private campgrounds during our first visit to any new area. While there we cruise the public campgrounds and, for those we find attractive, we fill out one of our **"Campground Scouting Report"** (included in Appendix A). We then file the forms by state in our growing collection of travel notes and observations. We also make note of the most spectacular sites both on our **"Report"** and in our daily RVing Journal.

Private Campgrounds – What Your Should Know. For the first time RVer, or for any RV traveler lacking in advance knowledge, private or commercial campgrounds are the surest bet. You will be less likely to wind up in a really outstanding camping spot, but you will also be much less likely to discover you have reserved a site which is too small, severely out of level, not accessible or otherwise unacceptable.

The largest single advantage to these campgrounds is that they offer a range of conveniences and facilities seldom found in the public campgrounds. If having a swimming pool or play ground would add to your experience, chances are there is a commercial campground in the area you are going which offers these. Electric, water, and often sewer hookups will be available. And a simple phone call will assure a campsite of adequate size and configuration for your unit.

These campgrounds are usually located close to interstate and other major highways (convenient, but noisy). Site width and privacy vary widely in commercial campgrounds – as do the quality and cleanliness of facilities. Commercial Campgrounds are almost always more expensive than their public counterparts. Fortunately there are readily available campground guides which will give you a good idea what to expect in terms of facilities, maintenance and cleanliness, and cost.

Conclusion: Your best bet is almost certainly to plan on staying in a commercial campground. If you find the RV lifestyle appealing and find yourself thinking about a return trip to the same area, then devote a bit of time to researching the other options – both public and private – when in the area. For now, don't stress about it. A comparatively minor bit of research will direct you to an acceptable commercial facility.

The research phase of campground selection is a simple task. Most of the work has already been done for you.

First there are the campground guides. The two largest and most comprehensive of these being **Woodall's** and the **Trailer Life Directory**. Each is around 2,000 pages long. We recommend you purchase a current issue of one or the other (we have both, but prefer the Trailer Life Directory) early in your planning process. At this introductory point in your life as an RVer there is really no reason to invest in both.

NOTE: Woodall's is available in smaller regional editions, but we recommend the larger, more comprehensive volume. Sentences starting with "What if" can be fun parts of your RV vacation . . . as in, "What if we went to the Florida Keys" or "What if we decided to tour the Oregon Coast". Having the complete national directory helps open your eyes to the possibilities and allows the browsing of campgrounds to be a part of the "what-ifing" process.

Both of the recommended guides have rating systems which give you a pretty good feel for the comparative qualities of various campgrounds. These directories also tell what facilities are available, give a range of costs based on the previous year's fees, include the dates the campground is open, and give you contact information and driving directions to the campground.

Other more specialized campground guides exist. We find these of varying degrees of usefulness. Two particularly good ones for our home state are those published by Foghorn Press titled "Colorado Camping" and by Westcliffe Publishers titled "Colorado Campgrounds, The 100 Best and All the Rest". The Foghorn guide rates the scenic beauty of each campground on a scale of 1 to 10. The Westcliffe book rates the campgrounds in a number of areas and focuses exclusively on public campgrounds. While each book is of value, both are probably in the "more than you need to know" category for the new RVer planning a first trip. The Woodall's or Trailer Life Directory will be sufficient.

$AVING$ TIP$

Don't Buy Both Woodall's and Trailer Life's Campground Directories. Look them over and buy which ever one you like best. The two are sufficiently similar to make having both pretty redundant. **NOTE:** For those who decide to join the Good Sam Club – only Trailer Life Directory identifies those campgrounds which give discounts to Good Sam members.

And Then There Are Web Forums. There are several very active RV Forums on the internet. We have provided web addresses for a few we have found particularly helpful in Appendix D. Web forums can be wonderful sources of additional information on RVing in general and on campgrounds specifically.

Try posting a message something like: "We are first time RVers and will be traveling in a 27 foot Class C to the Black Hills of South Dakota in mid-July. We are looking for campground recommendations and would appreciate input from members of this forum. Also, will we be able to 'plan as we go' or will we find reservations are necessary? Thanks in advance for your help!" Use these forums and tap into the expertise of those who have already "been there/done that". You will find the responses will be helpful.

In fact, as questions arise in your planning process, take advantage of the wealth of information available through these internet communities. You will find RVers to be a helpful bunch who enjoy welcoming and encouraging newcomers.

About the "R Word" – Reservations. Flexibility is a major advantage of RV travel. Extend a day in a special place, cut short your visit in another, or skip a destination altogether. Enjoying this flexibility is often done at a price. During peak seasons, a failure to plan may effectively eliminate the best, and in some areas all, of the campground options. Many campgrounds have overflow areas for last minute, unscheduled arrivals. These overflow areas are often just out in a field somewhere and are seldom the sorts of places where you would want to spend your vacation.

So, just how important are advance reservations? The admittedly unsatisfactory answer is "it depends". It depends on where you are traveling and when. It depends on where you want to stay – and on how particular you are about the quality of your site.

$AVING$ TIP$

Don't Pay Destination Rates for a Quick Overnight Stop. You will often have a choice between a nice destination type of campground with loads of facilities and a more Spartan, and less expensive, campground which offers little besides a place to park. Our previous tip recommended that you not pay for hookups which you don't need. Here we suggest that you not pay for facilities you are not going to have time to use. Avoid upscale campgrounds when all you really need is a parking place.

In general, if you are looking for a destination type of campground – a place where the success of your trip will depend as much on the time you spend hanging around the campground and joining in the activities there as on the time you are out running around playing tourist, give as much attention to arranging for your campground as possible. Give campground selection as much thought, research and planning as the selection of your RV. In living the RV life style, your surroundings – the out-of-doors – are often a more important a part of your living space than the interior of your RV.

Calling for reservations 6 months or even a year in advance is not an unreasonable thing to do when you want a really nice site in a high demand campground. Plan to spend a few extra minutes on the phone visiting with the person taking the reservation – placing yourself in their hands can greatly improve the odds of your getting a choice site.

Sometimes, even 6 or 8 months in advance is insufficient. By way of example, the Florida State Park System has some wonderful campgrounds in the Florida Keys. They also accept reservations 11 months in advance. Available sites are "released" at 8:00 AM Eastern Time. If you are looking for a particularly desirable site in a highly desirable campground during peak season, you will probably need to be flexible in your planned arrival date, you will have to be checking sites at exactly 8:00 AM Eastern Time 11 months to the day ahead of you planned arrival, and even then you will need a bit of luck. Oh, I know that 8:00 AM Eastern Time is 5:00 AM on the West Coast, but I can tell you that if you are so much as 10 minutes late your odds of getting a prime site will drop from very low to about zero.

On the other hand, don't overestimate the importance of your site if your intention is to stop in transit for one night only. If you wind up in a less than desirable campground (we have stayed in some real dumps – literally) remember that all campsites look alike when it's dark and the shades are pulled. You won't usually be impacted too much by a bad site on a brief, one night stop.

$AVING$ TIP$

Don't Pay for Hookups That You Don't Need. Most campgrounds offer a variety of campsite options. You will be offered a choice of sites with no hookups, with water and electric only, or with "full hookups". The tendency is to think, "Hey, I'm on vacation here. What the heck, give me the works!" Think about what hookups you actually need. You can usually stop at the campground's dump station to empty your holding tanks as you leave. Over a two week vacation, consistently paying for full hookups when you actually only need water and electric could easily cost you an extra $100.

THE IMPORTANCE OF "PLAN B"

In your planning process, try not to become too rigid. Leave some slack, plan some options. As you plan, remember that an inherent part of the planning process is the knowing that events which actually happen will differ from those which you have planned. These divergences will make your trip both interesting and frustrating. Think of your plan as a framework within which decisions can be made as you find out just how far off your plans are . . . and in what direction.

ALWAYS HAVE OPTIONS.

What will you do if the attraction you had planned to visit is, for whatever reason, closed. Or what if the place you go on Tuesday is so enjoyed by all you want to return on Wednesday? What if a neighbor in your campground tells you about a wonderful trail – will you have time to walk it? As you plan, build in the flexibility which will enable you to adjust your journey as you go. Insure you are able to take advantage of new information as it becomes available.

Bad Weather Blues? Not Necessarily! Nowhere is the importance of having options more obvious than in the general area of outdoor activities. The plan is to go for a hike on Monday. What will you do if Monday turns out to be a gloomy, rainy, cold, blustery sort of day? Such days can be problems for tenters . . . and memorable occasions for RVers. There are obvious foul weather options open to all: go to a museum, go to a movie, find a mall. There are also options uniquely available to RVers.

It is unlikely there is any place as snug or as cozy as the inside of an RV on a cold, rainy day. A wonderful place to cocoon! Fix a pot of soup or chili, microwave some popcorn, visit, play games, or just sit and read. The point is that bad weather days, with just a little planning, can become some of the most memorable of your RV experiment.

OK, your trip is planned. Or, at least to the extent you want it to be. Your schedule is penciled in, you know what you are renting and from whom. In short, the advance stuff is covered. Now, what do you need to know to actually live in an RV?

Chapter Seven
What Is On Board?
Tales of Systems & Stuff

We open this section by acknowledging that for many the most intimidating thing when considering an RV vacation is the RV itself. They seem so complex. There is so much to learn, to figure out, and to understand. Our intention here is to touch lightly, in a general introductory sort of way, on each of the major RV systems.

Your rental dealer will provide a thorough walk through and review of the specific systems in your unit. You are also likely to receive a fairly detailed manual instructing you in the operation of each system. Presented here is a highly condensed version of what you can expect.

SYSTEMS – STUFF THAT'S ATTACHED

To begin with know that your "house on wheels" has pretty much the same systems as your "house of sticks and bricks". Your RV is designed to do everything your house does plus a bit more . . . and to do so with a great deal of redundancy. Your sticks and stones house has a series of "systems" (a plumbing system, heating system, electrical system and so on) each designed for a specific function. You will find similar arrangements in your RV.

The information presented here is intentionally non-specific and is intended to serve as a prologue to the information you will be receiving from your dealer. Think of this section as providing a "heads up" – to bring your attention to those areas you will want to be certain are covered by your rental dealer.

SANITATION SYSTEM

What Is It & Why Is It Important?

As you live in your RV, you will generate liquid wastes through your sinks, the shower and the toilet. Your RV is designed with **HOLDING TANKS** where these wastes are collected. You will have a **BLACK WATER TANK**, where waste from the toilet is collected, and one or two **GRAY WATER TANKS** which will collect water from your sinks and shower.

Here's What You Should Know

Be sure you understand the process involved in "dumping" (emptying) these tanks. It is also important to find out how to monitor the levels of waste in these tanks and to make plans to empty them before they are totally full.

FRESH WATER

What Is It & Why Is It Important?

Your RV will have two fresh water systems – both of which will deliver water throughout your unit. You will have a large freshwater tank which you will fill as needed. This tank will use a 12-volt pump to deliver water throughout the RV. Additionally, there will be a place on the outside of your RV where you can attach a hose from an outlet at your campsite and provide pressurized water. It is generally a good idea to protect the RV's water system from surges in water pressure with a **PRESSURE REGULATOR**. Both the hose and the 12-volt pump provide water to the same places.

You will also have a **WATER HEATER**. Probably one which can operate either electrically or with propane. This water heater will provide hot water to all of those places where you would expect to find hot water – kitchen and bathroom sinks, shower, and outside shower if your unit has one.

Here's What You Should Know

You will want to know how to monitor your water levels in your fresh water tank, how to fill it when necessary, and how to connect to pressurized water. You will want to know how to turn your water pump off and on and will plan to have it turned off, unless specifically needed, when going down the road. Be sure your rental unit is equipped with a fresh water hose and if a pressure regulator is recommended or required, make sure one is included.

Water heaters are one of those things which somehow manage to be more confusing to operate than it seems they should. Be sure you understand how yours works! Also, water heaters use large amounts of propane. If yours has an option to run off of electricity, you might want to consider that option whenever you are plugged in to "shore power". If you must run your unit on propane, consider doing so only when hot water is actually needed – perhaps an hour or so each morning as an example. And, this is important, **NEVER RUN YOUR WATER HEATER WHEN YOU RV IS IN MOTION.**

$AVING$ TIP$

Don't Use "Your" Propane When You Can Use "Their" Electricity. Refilling your propane tank(s), while not horribly expensive, has both a time and a money cost. Several systems in your rental RV will operate with either electricity or propane – specifically your refrigerator and your water heater. Water heaters in particular consume massive amounts of propane. When in a campground and connected to "shore power" use "their" electricity, not your propane, to heat your water and run your refrigerator.

TIP: Think about propane levels before getting settled in for the evening. Virtually all systems for filling propane tanks involve your bringing your unit to the propane – the propane will seldom come to you. We have been known to plan poorly in this area, so we speak from experience in telling you it is highly exasperating to think you are done for the day only to find you have to unhook everything and go to some inconvenient place to get propane.

PROPANE

What Is It & Why Is It Important?

Your unit will have a propane tank of some sort which will provide fuel to fire your furnace, stove, water heater, and refrigerator. If this tank runs out of propane in the middle of a really cold, rainy night, you will be impressed at how quickly things cool off inside your unit.

Here's What You Should Know

SAFETY TIP: Your RV will shake and wiggle, bounce and jiggle as you go down the road. It stands to reason that a propane connection would be more likely to come loose during all this activity than with your rig sedately parked in a campground. That is why common sense (and the laws in many states) require you to turn off your propane at the tank while driving. Think of the possibilities: You could be heading down the road with your refrigerator operating on propane (or a pilot light on in the oven or on the stove). A propane line could separate. You would then be in the unenviable position of riding in a small can with an open flame as it rapidly fills with propane gas. The odds are that your RV will not develop a propane leak, but the point is that it could. Don't take an unnecessary chance. **ALWAYS TURN OFF YOUR PROPANE AT THE TANK WHILE DRIVING.**

Find out how to check your levels of propane (pretty much impossible if your unit doesn't have some sort of gauge for that purpose) and how your tank is filled. Many of the campgrounds you will be staying in sell propane. Those which don't will always know the closest place that does.

ALARMS & DETECTORS

TIP: RV Smoke Detectors are frequently located over the stove (Kay says this is proof RVs are designed by men). In the event you choose for some reason not to use your surprisingly loud and annoying exhaust fan when cooking bacon, this alarm will make enough noise to startle everyone in your RV and get the attention of all campers in adjacent sites. Be sure you learn how to quickly reset your Smoke Alarm.

What They Are & Why Are They Important?

Your unit should come equipped with a Carbon Monoxide Alarm, a Smoke and Fire Alarm, and a Propane/LP Alarm.

Here's What You Should Know

During your walk through, be sure to find out where each alarm and detector is located and how it works. These devices often seem like annoying details – at least until a time comes when they detect something and need to let you know about it. In those circumstances they can be of life saving significance.

ELECTRICAL

What Is It & Why Is It Important?

Take a couple who don't understand electricity (we would be an example of such a couple) and place them in an RV which operates with two different kinds of electricity which come from four different places and you are likely to have one very confused couple. Now, ask either of these people to explain all of this stuff they don't understand to someone who knows very little about RVs and you have created an opportunity for miscommunication. That pretty well describes where we are now.

We do not understand electricity. We assume it is working when the electrical stuff in our trailer operates more or less as we expect it to. When electrical things don't work, we know something very mysterious is going on (a failure to plug in whatever it is that is not working is a common source of the problem). If our explanation of RV electrical systems is less than clear, that is to be expected.

Various electrical things inside your RV will operate with one of two types of electricity – either 12-volt (lights, water pump, furnace blower, and the various exhaust fans and vents) or 120-volt (air conditioner, microwave and anything you plug into a standard outlet). This part seems fairly straight forward, but here's the thing: each of these types of electricity can come from two different places (there could be more for all we know, these are just the ones we recognize):

The sources of electricity for those things requiring 12-volts are either batteries (which will look either like automobile batteries or golf cart batteries) or via 120-volt electricity which first passes through a converter – whatever that is? As long as your batteries are charged, your 12-volt stuff will work. As long as your batteries are charged, it won't matter to your 12-volt stuff whether you are connected to some sort of 120-volt electricity or not. On the other hand, as long as your RV is plugged in to 120-volt electricity you don't need to be concerned about totally draining your batteries and finding yourself without electrical power.

Your 120-volt electricity will come from a generator (more on that in a moment) or from simply plugging your unit into an outlet (a concept which we do understand). RV parks have 20, 30 and sometimes 50 amp outlets. We have figured out that we don't need to understand the differences because it is impossible to plug one kind of cord into an inappropriate outlet. Your dealer will explain the sort of electricity your unit needs.

Here's What You Should Know

Fortunately, at least for some of us, electricity is one of those things you don't need to understand in order to use effectively. All you'll really need to know is where to find the cord you use to plug your unit into "shore power" and how do you use your monitor panel to check the levels of power remaining in you batteries. If your unit has a generator, you will want to know how to use it . . . and that is our next topic.

GENERATOR

What Is It & Why Is It Important?

Your unit is likely to come with a generator which can serve as a source of 120-volt power when you are unable to plug your unit in. There are a couple of situations where a generator is a convenience bordering on necessity:

The first which comes to mind is when you are driving down the road. On a day which is even a bit warm, you will find your automotive air is simply not enough to keep your unit comfortably cool. Your roof air conditioning unit requires 120-volt electricity. Know how to use your generator and you can drive down the road in comfort. Ignore your generator and those riding in back will suffer.

> **TIP:** Remember that some dealers charge a fee for the time you use the generator. Something on the order of $3.00 per hour is typical. (Other dealers include unlimited generator usage in their base rental fee.) This fee is normally small in the overall picture, but can be a big deal for those who insist on running their generators 24/7.

The other use for your generator is when you are stopped, need to run something requiring 120-volt electricity and don't have a place to plug in. You stop for lunch at a rest area and want to keep the air conditioner running – or use the microwave. You get into a campground late and find yourself in an overflow area. You choose a campground where hookups are unavailable.

Here's What You Should Know

Clearly a generator is a really handy thing to have when you need it. If your rental unit includes one, be sure you understand how to use it!

> **TIP 2:** If you have never slept in a tent next to an idiot who insisted on running his generator in the middle of the night, it may be difficult for you to understand how extremely annoying that is. In a campground, be considerate. Think of others before cranking up your generator. <u>Never run your generator during quiet hours</u>. At other times run it only when necessary. We have found when camping without hookups that running our generator for about an hour a day (usually mid-morning) is enough to keep our batteries charged. Anything else requiring 120-volt electricity, specifically hair dryers and microwave, we try to plan to use during that time.

AIR CONDITIONERS & VENTS

What Are They & Why Are They Important?

Your unit will most likely have an air conditioner. Additionally, there is likely to be an exhaust fan in the bathroom area and a vent fan over the stove. The air conditioner will require 120-volt electricity – either from having your unit plugged into shore power or from your generator. In the unlikely event your unit has a ceiling fan it will most probably operate from the 120-volt side of electrical possibilities. Other fans will almost certainly be 12-volt.

Here's What You Should Know

We once stayed at Dead Horse Point State Park in Moab, UT for a few days in early June. There was electricity at our site, but our air conditioner wasn't working. Daily highs were is the mid 90s and it felt like 110. It was perhaps our most miserable trip since moving out of tents. The point is that RVs heat up really, really fast on hot days and can be pretty miserable. In the creation of a memorable trip – memorable in a good sort of way – your air conditioner can be your best friend.

FURNACES & HEATERS

What Are They & Why Are They Important?

Furnaces are pretty much self explanatory. Your unit will most likely have a residential type of thermostat and your furnace will run on propane and 12 volt electricity.

Here's What You Should Know

So long as you monitor your propane level, your furnace shouldn't give you much trouble. If you do have a problem – with your furnace or with anything else in your RV for that matter – your first, best bet is to ask a neighbor. We will talk more about that in a moment, but for now know that RVers generally are friendly and extraordinarily helpful. All remember when they were new and are anxious to welcome others to the life style.

$AVING$ TIP$

Furnaces use a massive amount of propane. Additionally, their blowers can be a bit disruptive as they cycle on and off, on and off, on and off throughout the night. We typically turn our furnace off at night. We use an electric blanket when we have hookups, a down comforter when we don't. (Such bedding is perhaps impractical when you are doing a fly/drive rental, but otherwise is a thing to consider.) First one up in the morning turns on the furnace and comes back to bed while it runs through one or two cycles.

Also, consider a small electric heater. These are inexpensive – most assuredly cheaper than a tank of propane – and, while they won't heat your entire unit, they can do a wonderful job of warming things up a few degrees. Sometimes that can make all the difference.

OTHER STUFF

Generally there are two kinds of stuff to deal with on your RV adventure. There is stuff which is an attached, integral part of your RV. We have just finished a light overview of those sorts of things.

Beyond the attached, know that pretty much anything you can think of is being carried around in someone's RV somewhere in North America. In **Appendix B** we have provided a couple of checklists to give you a bit of direction as you think about what to bring along on your RV vacation.

As a starting point, assume that, unless you have made specific arrangements, you will find no unattached stuff in your rental RV. Some general discussion is in order:

Bedding is one of the things you won't generally find as a standard inclusion in a rental RV. We don't know why that is so, only that it is. Motels/hotels wouldn't consider renting a room without bedding, in the RV rental business it is considered normal. We would think that someone would have realized those of us paying $1,000 or so for a one week rental will tend to spend a portion of our time sleeping . . . and that our sleeping experience would be enhanced by the addition of perhaps a pillow and a sheet. Such is not the case.

Tips, Tricks & Techniques: Your RV, depending on its size and on the size of your traveling party, will likely have areas which serve multiple purposes. Specifically, dinettes and sofas which at night convert to beds. Those who choose a Class C Motorhome will also have a cab over area which they may choose to leave set up as a bed.

This now it's a bed and now it's not sort of thing can become a bit tiresome. For that reason, many RVers – both owners and renters – use sleeping bags in these convertible areas. A sleeping bag, a pillow and perhaps a sheet simplifies the process of sleeping in a dinette.

> **More Tips, Tricks & Techniques:** An aside here to note that we very, very seldom use the shower in our RV. For one thing, our shower is always full of assorted stuff. (You will find a dry shower a handy place to throw those bulky sleeping bags, pillows and other bedding when your unit is in its day-time configuration). We have found the showers in RV Parks generally (but not always) clean and of adequate size. Acceptable water pressure and a sufficient supply of hot water are the norms.

Yours or Theirs? Most dealers offer, for an additional $30 to $40 per person, some form or another of a package of bedding and other personal items like towels and wash cloths (which may help to explain why such items are not included in your $200 a day RV rental and are found in a $65.00 motel room).

The question is one of using the dealers stuff or your own. The answer is to do whichever is the most convenient for you. If you are renting your unit locally, and if you have sleeping bags and appropriate bedding, we suggest you use your own. On a fly/drive rental, pay the extra and let the dealer provide the bedding.

Bath Supplies, Towels, etc.

The same line of reasoning which provides beddingless beds extends to the bathroom where we find a sink and a shower, but no towels or wash cloths.

Yours or Theirs? Deciding who provides the wash cloths and towels is a pretty straight forward issue. If you are renting "personal packages" (bedding) from your dealer, towels and washcloths are typically included. If you are providing your own bedding, you will need to plan on providing your own towels and wash cloths.

Kitchen Equipment

By this point in our little review, it will come as no surprise that your RV will have a kitchen, in which you are given no way of cooking, and a table at which you could eat, at least in theory, if you were supplied some sort of plates and utensils, which of course you are not.

Critical Kitchen Stuff. Your kitchen and the area of cooking – or not – on your vacation is a large subject and of enough importance that we have devoted the following chapter to it. For now, suffice it to say that your dealer will also offer, at additional cost (are you starting to see a pattern here?) a semi-adequate package of kitchen equipment for those whose desire is to do a semi-adequate job of meal preparation.

Other Inside Stuff

Your RV is not likely to come equipped with a TV, VCR or a Stereo System beyond that which is built into the dash. If you see this as a problem, discuss it with your dealer. They may have some rental entertainment equipment available . . . or the dealer may be able to give you some input as to what others have done.

$AVING$ TIP$

Equip Your RV With Stuff You Already Own. Loading an RV with stuff you buy and with stuff you rent from the dealer is simply a lot more expensive than filling it up with stuff you find around the house. The best, and cheapest, way to load a rental RV is to park it in your own driveway and toss in things which seem important until the RV is "properly equipped" – as defined by you.

Consider bringing some board games, a deck of cards, a few books, some sports equipment and other alternative forms of entertainment. For both adults and children, an important part of the vacation experience can be doing things you don't normally do.

Outside Stuff

A significant reason many choose an RV vacation is the opportunity to simply enjoy being outdoors. Being outdoors means different things to different people. We for example have spent some of our most memorable RV moments sitting in the shade, pretending to read a no-brainer sort of book, while watching the day slide by. In a continuation of the minimalist approach to RV outfitting, your unit is unlikely to come with lawn chairs or sporting equipment or a charcoal grill or a table cloth for your picnic table.

Give thought, in advance, to the sorts of things you think you'd like to be able to do outside your RV. Talk to your dealer – they may have optional items for rent for your use outside. If not, your dealer has seen countless other RV renters with desires for experiences similar to those you are seeking. The dealer's job is to help you have the best RV vacation possible. They can offer guidance if you simply ask.

Much Miscellaneous & Loads of Etcetera

Remember your RV will be your home on wheels. Think about those things which, as defined by you, would enhance your experience. Make plans to bring whatever is appropriate . . . and more.

Of all forms of vacation travel, RVing is the most sympathetic of those compelled to travel with excess stuff. We love to read and, when RVing, we consistently bring three or four times as many books as we could possibly read in the time available. Why? Because having many books gives us options. The ability to bring excess books relieves us of the need to decide today what sorts of things we will be in the mood to read two weeks from now.

In closing, we should perhaps apologize for our comments about the standard lack of equipment in most rental RVs. Perhaps we should, but we don't think so. You pay big bucks to rent a cabin or a condo, and it is assumed you will want to eat and sleep in it – it is equipped accordingly. You pay big bucks to rent a motel room, and it is assumed you will want to sleep in it – it is equipped accordingly. You pay big bucks to rent an RV with places to sleep and a kitchen, and it is assumed you should pay extra if you want to use either. It is a position which doesn't make sense to us.

Chapter Eight
The Rental RV Kitchen

The kitchen, or galley, is arguably the most controversial area in the rental RV. Love it or hate it, use it or ignore it, the fact is a small kitchen will be traveling with you on your vacation. This chapter is intended for those who are considering using the kitchen they will be hauling around.

$AVING$ TIP$

Minimize Eating Out. The more serious you are about saving money, the more you may want to take advantage of your RVs kitchen. Prepare a special meal or two, each in a special place, and you can add great memories to your RV vacation even as you are saving money.

GENERAL COMMENTS

There is a group of RV vacationers, we'll call this one the "I'm not going on any vacation where I have to cook" group, who are disappointed to find kitchens of any sort in their home on wheels. That a kitchen will actually be following along, uninvited, on their vacation seems somehow unfair.

At the other end of the range of opinion we find the "kitchen is the heart of the household" group. This group finds concern in the minimalist nature of RV kitchens. How, they wonder, are they ever to prepare adequate meals in a kitchen which seems less than fully present?

In the eyes of the anti-cooking group, the pro-cooking group appears at least a few tablespoons short of a full cup. The pro-cooking group leans towards a belief that their non-cooking counterparts are overlooking one of the most potentially pleasurable areas of an RV vacation.

Between these two extremes we find the majority of RV vacationers. The majority doesn't have strong opinions about cooking and vacationing. They assume they will cook when it is convenient and eat out when it is not. To this group a minimalist kitchen, one which seems neither fully present nor totally absent, is as it should be.

An RV vacation presents alternatives you don't have on more conventional trips. Included in the range of options is the choice to eat out as much, or as little, as you like. RV kitchens exist to give you that freedom.

EQUIPPING

We know the kitchen in your rental RV will be under sized and under equipped. Whether or not that matters is a separate question. If you intend to use your RV's kitchen at all, there are some things you need to find out:

Be Very Clear, In Advance, What Is Included in Your Unit. Exactly what will be in your RV's kitchen? Don't, for example, make the mistake of showing up with a take and bake pizza for your first night on the road unless you are certain you have an oven (you probably won't). Will your unit have a stove and refrigerator? (almost certainly) A microwave? (highly likely). Basic utensils? (almost certainly not).

Given there is a logic in the RV rental industry which finds it makes sense to provide beds with no bedding and showers with no towels, you would expect your kitchen to be non-functional . . . and you would be right. Unless you make specific arrangements it is a virtual certainty you will find no equipment of any kind in your kitchen – not as much as a single skillet.

Just how does the rental RV vacationer start with a kitchen which is both small and empty and wind up able to prepare a meal? What sort of stuff is needed? And where will it come from? Because RV vacations are taken by individuals with differing needs and objectives, there is no single, simple answer to the "how" and "with what" of equipping rental RV kitchens.

There are two major variables and an infinite number of minor issues. The first consideration is to ask yourself exactly how seriously you are planning to take this whole meal preparation idea. The second major point is whether you are renting your unit locally or planning a fly/drive vacation. We suggest a sort of middle ground approach to equipping your RV's kitchen – don't go with the intent of being a gourmet on wheels, but do plan to prepare a few things that are at least moderately interesting.

On a fly/drive trip your easiest option (easiest, but not necessarily the best or the cheapest) is to rent your kitchen equipment from the same dealer where you are renting your RV. These equipment packages go by a variety of names (provisioning kit, kitchen kit) and typically cost in the $75 to $100 range for the length of your trip. These kits tend to be pretty minimal both as to inclusions and as to quality. Ask your dealer for more details.

The Two Pan Gourmet. You won't need a lot of stuff. A two pan approach will work well in your RV kitchen and should be considered whether you are equipping a unit parked in your driveway or are flying to some far away place to meet up with an empty kitchen. Plan to have one fairly **large, non-stick covered skillet** (something around 12 inches would be perfect) and a **moderate size sauce pan with lid** (3 quarts will work for most traveling groups).

Those loading an RV parked in their driveway will be best served by selecting pans from their own kitchens, pans with which they are both familiar and comfortable. If equipping a fly/drive unit, know that at the time of this writing the pans recommended here can be purchased at Wal-Mart for $18.94 and $17.83 respectively.

A Slow Cooker May Be Your Most Valued Appliance. If your travel plans have penciled in time when your RV will be remaining "on site" for a day (or several days), and if you are loading your RV in your driveway, consider putting in a slow cooker.

Slow cookers are useful for those with a separate vehicle to drive around during the day, or when planning an all day commercial tour (leaving from the campground), or when a day is set aside as a "stay at home day". In short, any time your rig will be staying in place for an entire day (with electrical hookups) is potentially a slow cooker sort of day. Returning from a full day of hiking or sightseeing or shopping to a "home-on-wheels" filled with the smells of a ready to eat dinner is a pleasure available in few other modes of travel.

Consider a "Big Sky Bistro". For many of us the notions of camping and coffee are ideas which are inseparably joined. If you are in that category, consider taking along a **"Big Sky Bistro"** or two. These units combine the brewing power of a traditional French press coffee maker with the durability of a plastic thermal coffee mug. So long as you have some ground coffee and a way to boil water, your Bistro will produce an excellent mega-cup of brew. Simply scoop in three or four tablespoons (medium grind) of your favorite bean, heat water nearly to boiling and pour to within an inch or so of the top, and cover with the lid-and-plunger assembly. Steep for about four minutes and push down the plunger. You can drink your 16 ounces of fresh brewed mixture straight from the mug. It will stay hot seemingly forever. Find yours nationwide at outdoor stores or online at www.porterproducts.com.

Pay Attention to What You Cook With At Home – By far the best way to figure out what kitchen stuff you'll want to have with you on your RV vacation is to pay attention to what you really use at home. Starting at least a couple of weeks before your trip, place a note pad on your kitchen counter. Each time you use something jot it down. You will quickly find there are some things you had been considering for your RV kitchen that you never really use. There will be others you perhaps hadn't thought of and yet find you actually use several times a day. Space is at a premium in your RV, don't waste it by filling it up with things you somehow feel you "should" use – not when you have proven you don't.

You will find a list titled **"Basic Kitchen Inventory"** in Appendix B. As you would expect, this form is not all inclusive; however, it should provide you with a great starting point as you think about what to put in your RV kitchen.

THE KITCHEN ANNEX

Perhaps the most important concept in our view of an RV kitchen is the notion of its extending beyond the walls of the RV. Our kitchen includes the picnic table, a grill, and often a campfire. Collectively these areas are what we call "The Kitchen Annex". (We could of course call them "the picnic table, the grill and the campfire", but that somehow seems less interesting.) We prepare far more meals in our annex than inside our RV. We encourage you to also think of your RV's kitchen as being a space which continues beyond the physical walls of your RV.

Why It's Important: The Kitchen Annex is important first because the point of an RV vacation is to do more than hang out inside your RV. If sitting around inside were your primary objective, you could simplify the process, and save a few bucks in gas money, by renting an RV and leaving it in your driveway. Accepting the concept of a kitchen annex brings you outside in the fresh air where you can really experience the area you've chosen for your vacation.

A second argument favoring the concept of a Kitchen Annex is the understanding there are some meals which it is not wise to prepare in small, enclosed spaces. The odors of cooking cabbage and fish – a couple of obvious examples – can linger for days.

Finally, food prepared and consumed out-of-doors, spiced with fresh air and sunshine, simply tastes better.

Equipping The Annex: Let's take a look at three areas you might want to consider for inclusion in your RV's Kitchen Annex.

The Campfire: For many "campsite", "camping" and "campfire" are all under the same umbrella of experience. A high portion of our readers first experienced camp cooking in the burning of hotdogs and marshmallows over an open fire.

Most privately owned campgrounds do not allow campfires, but some do. Most public campgrounds do allow campfires, but some don't. The point here is to first find out if campfires are an option where you will be staying. If so, preparing even a crude meal while gathered around the campfire can make for exceptional memories.

Campfire cooking can be as complex or as simple as you want it to be. We personally tend towards the complex end of the spectrum with tripods and cooking grates and camp style Dutch ovens and a variety of cast iron cookware all for cooking over campfires. The RV renter would be better served by keeping it simple. If desiring to try some campfire cooking, bring a few **long handled roasting forks** designed for cooking hot dogs and marshmallows. Bring some **heavy duty aluminum foil**. Period. Don't get too carried away with any aspect of cooking while on your RV vacation – and that includes campfire cooking.

The Grill: Some campsites will include some sort of basic grill, some won't. Again, the point is to find out in advance. Don't allow a situation where you arrive planning to do steaks on the grill only to find out there is no grill. Depending on the sort of life-style you plan for your RV vacation, you may find the purchase of an inexpensive, basic sort of **charcoal grill** and a **bag of charcoal** to be worthwhile.

> ### $AVING$ TIP$
>
> **A Small Inexpensive Charcoal Grill** and a bag of easy light charcoal combine to inexpensively add a great cooking alternative for your vacation meals. A few commercial campgrounds will have grills, most will not. Most public campgrounds will have grills, a few won't. A small, round grill is really cheap and will allow you a grilling option even in a campsite where no grill is provided.

We carry a Porta Chef Propane Grill by Broil King – wonderful for our purposes, but too large and too expensive for the purposes of the RV renter. Get something cheap, a **spray bottle** of some sort for water to control flare-ups, and **something you can use to turn hamburgers**, chicken, steaks and hot dogs. Again, keep it simple. If you find yourself with a lasting case of "hitch itch" and decide to get more involved in the RV life style, there will be ample opportunity to upgrade the grilling portion of your Kitchen Annex.

An Outside Stove: This area of the Kitchen Annex is a tricky one. Complicated because there really isn't a convenient, easy, throw away type of option here. If you are equipping your unit from your home base, and if you already own a two burner Coleman type of stove or an electric skillet . . . consider bringing one of them along. We probably would not go out and buy either just for the purpose of cooking a very few meals on a single trip.

Having said that, we also note that we use our outdoor stove(s) far, far more than the one inside. In fact, other than as a place to heat water for coffee, tea or hot chocolate, we very seldom – make that very, very seldom – cook inside unless we are making a quick, one night stop or unless insects or weather force us inside. We carry two different two burner propane stoves and an electric skillet – all for use in our annex. (We understand we are over equipped by the standards of most, but hey, that's part of the attraction of RV travel – you don't have to be reasonable about the amounts of stuff you want to haul around.)

STOCKING THE PANTRY

Here is another area where less is better. For starters, if you are not sure when you are going to eat it, don't carry it around. Leave room for those interesting local specialties – pinon coffee in the Southwest or maple syrup in the Northeast. Such extras such add both fun to your trip and depth to your memories after you return home.

Shop Like You Would At Home. You will be well served by stocking your pantry with those things you would buy if you were home – only less. It is fun to experiment with new foods and new ways of doing things. It is at least equally true that too many experiments which deviate from your family's definition of food can leave you with an RV full of hungry, grumpy people.

Our advice on stocking the pantry is to not overdo it. Keep in mind that everyplace you go there will be people . . . and pretty much all of those people eat. Which means there will also be grocery stores wherever you go. Admittedly, you may find prices a bit higher than you are used to, but it is at least equally expensive to go out and buy a lot of food for your pantry which you don't eat.

$AVING$ TIP$

Bring your own snacks. Your rental RV comes with a refrigerator and cupboards. Set them up as your snack and drink sources. Roadside convenience stores tend to offer snacks which are both more expensive and nutritionally inferior to those you can pack yourself. When the time comes to replenish your snack supplies, do so at a major supermarket or a discount warehouse – not at a convenience store.

You have intentionally built in opportunities for choice by under scheduling/under planning your travel itinerary. It is equally important to leave room for flexibility in your meal planning. You may create situations where you need to make an extra grocery stop or two, but what the heck, you never know what interesting local stuff you might find as you wander around in a strange market.

The Spice Bag. One area of pantry stocking where we feel it wise to be oversupplied is in the selection of spices. Generally speaking, spices are expensive and have limited shelf lives, but you already have the spices you most frequently use in your cupboard at home. Throw a dozen of your favorites – you know which ones they are – in a resealable plastic bag. Spices are a cost effective and space efficient way to add variety to your RV meals.

And don't just carry those spices around, use them. Try rubbing a steak with a bit of olive oil and sprinkling it with garlic salt before grilling, put a pinch of cinnamon in your coffee or hot chocolate, or a dash of chili powder in your scrambled eggs. You get the idea! Don't leave home without your **spice bag**. Nothing adds depth and interest to your RV meals as quickly as the intelligent application of appropriate seasonings.

$AVING$ TIP$

Bring a "Spice Bag". A "Spice Bag" is a low cost way to add interest to your RVing meals. Simply gather up a dozen or so of the spices you most like to cook with and toss them into a re-sealable plastic bag. A dozen spices take up so little room that the Spice Bag is even a practical addition for the fly/drive RVer.

Try Local Specialties. Wherever you travel, there will be local specialty foods. To the extent you are able to incorporate these foods into your meal planning you will be doing more to absorb the area you have traveled to experience. Using local foods may require a bit of extra thought, but you will find great depth is added to your feel for the area.

MEAL PLANNING

For those times you do decide to cook, keep your meal plans simple. Organize around these guiding principals: Never miss a sunset because you are inside cooking. <u>NEVER</u>. Never find yourself excluded from what the rest of your party is doing because you are inside cooking. <u>NEVER</u>. Finally, whenever possible, move the entire meal preparation process outside to the Kitchen Annex.

To whatever extent you decide to cook, insist on simplicity as your guiding principal. You will be working in a small, poorly equipped kitchen and working from a small, poorly stocked pantry. That's just the way it is.

Quick and Easy is the Key. The simple nature of your kitchen facilities, and the assumption your trip is intended as a vacation and not as a traveling dining experience, suggest meals which are both quick and easy. In our opinion, you should not be considering meals requiring more ingredients than you can carry through the express lane, nor recipes requiring more than 30 minutes prep time.

"Quick and easy" need not be synonymous with "bland and boring". In testing for our soon to be released book "Fast & Fabulous Recipes for the RV Kitchen" we were able to come up with a wonderful variety of interesting recipes – all requiring only a limited pallet of ingredients and less than 30 minutes prep time.

Dining al fresco. Do consider that meal times provide an opportunity to provide another layer of experiences to your RV adventure. This need not mean a meal far from your norm, nor does it require complex or elaborate preparation – though it could.

If it is your family routine to have pizza every Sunday night, consider Sunday night pizza while on your RV vacation. Perhaps some take-out pizza under the pines on a not quite level picnic table. For as far as you can see into the future, each Sunday night's pizza will cause all to remember your RV vacation.

Or try this: Buy a take-out meal of local specialties. Bring it all back to your site and eat it at that same rustic table. A self-catered memory!!

Obviously you can plan to cook something special, just remember to keep it simple. Look to meal possibilities which can be prepared over a campfire or on a charcoal grill. Add a few unusual extras to a hamburger or hot dog (we have included a sample recipe for each) and turn simple fare into an unforgettable meal.

As previously mentioned, one way of adding depth to your vacation experience is to have a special meal in an extraordinary spot. If your campground doesn't seem particularly scenic, watch for RV accessible picnic areas as you tour the area. You are an RVer now and your kitchen and pantry a will be with you wherever you go.

A word of caution: many picnic grounds are not designed with large vehicles in mind. Before pulling into any area in your RV, be sure you first see how you are going to be able to get out – and backing a huge RV down a long, narrow, winding road is seldom a good plan. Also, note that in some wooded picnic areas overhead clearance can be an issue. Remember, your RV is a lot taller than anything you are used to driving.

$AVING$ TIP$

If You Do Eat Out, Have Your Main Meal At Lunchtime. It is cheaper to eat out at noon than in the evening. Doing so has the added advantage of leaving your evenings free to enjoy the amenities of your campground and the RV lifestyle you set out to experience.

KITCHEN CONCLUSIONS

RV adventures have this in common: We load up some stuff, go a few places, do some things and then return (or continue on to other places). The point of these travels may be simply the creation of enduring memories.

As we journey, we can choose to create experiences with a bit of style, a touch of eccentricity, an unexpected elegance. In short, we can each choose to do things in our own special way and can create vacations which occupy unique places in memory. The more unusual our experiences, the more intense are our memories. One way of creating truly singular memories is to enjoy an unordinary meal in a special place.

"Unordinary" need not mean complicated, difficult or time consuming to prepare. The following are a few ideas to stimulate your thinking.

As an RVer, you have rejected conventional means of travel. Why should you settle for ordinary food? A special meal does not have to involve extensive preparations or missing a sunset because you are slaving away in the RV kitchen. It can be as simple as flowers on the picnic table, hamburgers on pewter plates instead of paper, or a Bacon Blue Cheese Burger instead of an ordinary hamburger.

Recipes

Deluxe Campfire Dogs

hot dogs (assume two per person)
onion slices (thin slices)
cheese (small wedges)
mustard (optional)
catsup (optional)
uncooked bacon (1 strip per hot dog)

Split hot dogs lengthwise (only about ¾ of the way through).

Put a thin piece of onion and/or cheese into the slit in each hot dog. Add a little catsup and/or mustard.

Wind one strip of bacon firmly around each hot dog and secure with a couple of toothpicks.

Using a roasting fork, cook over campfire coals until bacon is crisp.

Remove from roasting fork, <u>pull out the toothpicks</u>, and serve on a warmed bun.

You are going to eat anyway, so why not make the occasion memorable?

Bacon Blue Cheese Burgers

6 Servings

2	Pounds	Ground Beef
2	Tablespoons	Lemon Zest
3	Tablespoons	Lemon Juice
1	Cup	Blue Cheese (Crumbled)
		Salt
		Coarsely Ground Pepper
6	Slices	Bacon (Crisply Fried)
		Barbeque Sauce

Prepare and measure all ingredients before starting to cook.

Combine ground beef, lemon zest, and lemon juice in a large bowl. Mix thoroughly. Add Blue Cheese and toss lightly.

Shape ground beef mixture into 6 patties, each about 1 inch thick.

If time permits, refrigerating the patties for about an hour will make them firmer and easier to handle on the grill.

Sprinkle each burger with salt and fresh, coarsely ground, black pepper.

Charcoal Grill: Grill burgers uncovered directly over medium coals until meat juices run clear and meat is not long pink in the center – about 6 to 8 minutes per side – turning once. During the final minute or two, top each burger with a slice of previously fried bacon. Gas Grill: Preheat grill. Adjust heat to medium. Place burgers over direct heat. Cover and grill as with charcoal.

Remove burgers from grill. Serve immediately on a bed of fresh lettuce. Drizzle with your favorite barbeque sauce.

NOTE: We originally developed this recipe for inclusion in a collection of low carb recipes and intended it to be served with low carb barbeque sauce. If you are not concerned about carbs, serve these on traditional hamburger buns which you have first lightly toasted on your grill.

You are going to eat anyway, so why not make the occasion memorable?

"Go Box" Skillet Chicken

2 Servings

¼	cup	butter
¼	cup	olive oil
1	clove	garlic (minced)
7	ounces	canned mushroom slices (1 can)
¼	cup	dried parsley
1	cup	water
1	teaspoon	chicken bouillon granules
12½	ounces	canned chicken (about 1 cup)
4	ounces	spaghetti, cooked and drained
		Grated Parmesan (optional)

Prepare and measure all ingredients before starting to cook.

Melt butter in 12" skillet over medium heat, add olive oil and heat for about 5 minutes.

Add garlic and mushrooms. Sauté for 3 minutes. Add parsley, water, and chicken bouillon granules. Bring mixture to a boil.

Reduce heat and simmer uncovered for 10 minutes.

Add canned chicken and simmer for another 10 minutes.

Serve chicken mixture over hot spaghetti. Top with grated Parmesan (optional).

You are going to eat anyway, so why not make the occasion memorable?

AUTHORS' NOTE:

We are developing a series of cookbooks specifically for RV Kitchens. These books focus on the preparation of interesting food while operating with the space and equipment limitations of an RV kitchen . . . and with the limited pallet of ingredients available in an RV pantry.

The first of these is simply titled **"RV Kitchens"**. It is THE complete guide to equipping, stocking and working in an RV Kitchen. Included in this book are 104 RV tested recipes (enough to sample two new recipes each week for a year) and a bonus section with a dozen unique recipes for campfire cooking. Each of these RV friendly recipes has what it takes to create memories which will linger long after your RV Rental Vacation has come to a close.

For detailed information about the **"RV Kitchens"** book, and/or to subscribe to the free **"RV Kitchens eZine"**, visit our web sites at www.RVRentalGuide.com and www.RVKitchens.com. **You are not going on an ordinary vacation, don't settle for ordinary food!**

Dealing with the notion of an RV kitchen has moved most of our readers to unfamiliar ground. Those with backgrounds in other sorts of self-contained travel, specifically back packing and car camping, will find the RV kitchen expansive and liberating. Those with backgrounds in other forms of travel are likely to have previously given the idea of a traveling kitchen and its accompanying pantry somewhere between very little and no thought at all.

The remainder of the process of packing (actually we think of it as "loading") for an RV vacation will find all on more familiar ground. Packing for an RV vacation for most of our readers will be packing like they are used to – only more so. In the case of those who are renting locally, and loading in their driveways, it will be packing as usual, only <u>much</u> more so.

Chapter Nine
What Should We Bring?

*L*oading for an RV vacation is different, in both quantity and content, than packing for previous non-RV trips you may have taken. It is not realistic to expect that you, as a first time RVer, will "pack perfectly". To do so would require perfect foresight. (We also note it is also unlikely you will "pack perfectly" for your 30th RV trip; however, as you gain experience you can expect to make fewer errors of consequence.) We urge you to give the material in this chapter some thought – to include the thinking of others who have "been there, done that" as you decide what to bring along on your RV vacation. At a minimum, you will reduce the number of really important things you leave behind!

If packing is so important, why is this chapter so short? The simple answer is to repeat that the choice to go on an RV vacation is a lifestyle decision. In selecting an RV vacation, the traveler is saying, "I'm tired of my vacations being planned and scheduled by others. This time I want to do things my way." To do things "your way" requires that the packing/loading process focus on including things defined as important by you and of excluding those things which you assume will not add to your experience.

We could provide detailed packing checklists (and we have done so in our workbook **"Travel Planning for RV Renters"**); however, any checklists provided by us are by definition reflective of those things we define as important. We believe your trip will be more satisfactory if you work from lists which are specific to your way of doing things.

$AVING$ TIP$

Don't Buy Special Equipment. As you begin to get ready for your first ever RV trip, it is tempting to start thinking about all the special equipment you "need". The truth is that, beyond what you'll get from your RV rental dealer, you don't "need" any of it. If you are serious about keeping your vacation affordable, resist the temptation to go out and buy boxes full of gadgets. (On the other hand, a couple of totally frivolous items can be a lot of fun.)

A TWO PART PROCESS

The process of packing/loading for an RV trip is one which starts where packing for a more conventional sort of trip would be finishing. Packing/loading for an RV adventure can, for the RV renter, be viewed as a two step process:

Start in a familiar place. Pack first as if you were going on a casual, outdoorsy, conventional sort of vacation. One where you fly to your destination. (If you are doing a "fly/rent" sort of RV vacation, this may also be where you stop packing . . . or where you turn to some of the more "creative" options we cover in **Chapter 12: Special Considerations - Fly/Drive RV Rentals**.)

The second phase of selecting "stuff" to bring along on your RV adventure is the area where many see the first measurable benefit in the RV lifestyle. In this phase you begin to add those things which you would have liked to have included on your previous travels, but left behind due to space considerations. As you begin the selection of this "Phase 2 Stuff" you will quickly notice lifestyle differences – both in "what" you pack and, perhaps more importantly, in the area of "how much" you decide to bring along.

A Journey to the Florida Keys. A few years ago, we were preparing for what was to be our longest RV trip to that point – in terms of both times and distance (we drove from Denver to Key West and back and were gone 38 days). It was also our first extended trip in a new fifth wheel – a trailer which has a large wardrobe extending across the entire front of the trailer.

About a month before our scheduled departure Kay started carrying clothes out to the trailer. Not just a single outfit or a couple of t-shirts – great arm loads of clothes. The process continued day after day after day. Eventually Dave's curiosity got the best of him, "What is the plan here? Are you just taking everything you own to Florida or what?"

Kay looked at him with as much seriousness as she is capable of focusing on one who has just asked an incredibly stupid question, "Could you tell me *exactly* what the point would be in taking an empty closet all the way to Florida?" The logic preempted any response Dave might have had in mind.

General Observations. Her point is a good one. Empty or full, the closet was going to Florida that much was clear. Equally true is that there was no advantage in its being empty.

So here's the thing: When comparing RV travel to travel by airline, the standard "two suitcases not to exceed 50 pounds each" becomes a starting point rather than a limiting factor. Those loading at home tend to continue carrying stuff out to their RV until it becomes clear that no empty closets (or drawers or cupboards) will be accompanying them on their trip.

Even those doing a fly/rent sort of trip tend to expand far beyond the airlines view of "reasonable" as they continue along on a trip of one week or more. I venture to say that it is more common than not for fly/rent RVers to find themselves with one or more boxes of "extra stuff" which they ship home at the end of their trip.

CLOTHING CONSIDERATIONS

Think Casual & Comfortable. When RVing, casual dress is the custom, the norm. Casual and comfortable. An interesting dichotomy in RVing is that, more than any other travel style, you are able to bring excessive quantities of clothing and yet there may be no style of travel in which there is less need for a diversified wardrobe.

There is of course no rule against "dressing up" in RV travel. You have room for the clothing and may enjoy dressing for an evening out now and then. *There Is No Rule Against "Dressing Up"* . . .

but Few People Do. You will find that upscale clothing is an exception to custom.

$AVING$ TIP$

Don't Buy Special Clothing. Unlike trips you may have taken in the past, RV vacations don't require any special clothing. Casual and comfortable – that's the RV lifestyle. If you plan to go out to someplace special, you might bring one outfit that's a bit upscale. Otherwise, think casual and comfortable as you pack and your wardrobe will be perfect.

Think Casual, Comfortable, Flexible. If there is a "rule" for putting together an RVing wardrobe, it is that it be casual, flexible and, above all else, comfortable. We have <u>never</u>, in all our decades of RVing, been in an RV related situation where casual clothing was inappropriate. If it makes your feel better, take one outfit which is a sort of "up-scale casual". It is unlikely you will need it.

As in packing for any trip, think in terms of flexibility. Dave's rule of thumb is to not take anything unless it can be worn at least three different ways. (As an aside, Kay finds such criteria to be more bother than value.) You will save yourself some aggravation by selecting a wardrobe which is easy to care for and not inclined to wrinkle. Additionally, let your selection process favor darker colored clothing. White slacks might look great on a cruise ship, but they won't look good for more than about 5 minutes hanging around a campfire.

Be Prepared For Changing Weather. Occasionally you will go on an RV trip and find you have perfect weather from start to finish. While it could happen on the trip you are now planning, our advice is to not count on it. Yours is likely to be an active trip with an orientation towards outdoor activities. Pack in such a way as to be prepared for changes in weather.

If you are too cold, too hot or too wet, it is at best difficult to enjoy your vacation. Dressing in **layers** instead of in a single, heavy piece of clothing allows you to adjust to a variety of weather conditions. Assuming you will not be taking your RV vacation during extremely cold weather, you will be well served by an outer layer which is of a breathable, wind and water proof material worn over a middle layer of insulating material such as a fleece jacket or a sweater.

Finally, the ability to bring along more clothing than you need doesn't mean there is a requirement that you do so. In fact, you can choose the "keep it simple" school of thought and bring a minimal amount of clothing. Nearly all commercial RV parks have coin-operated laundry facilities.

THE COMFORTS OF HOME

A unique aspect of RV travel is the extent to which the experience can be personalized. Nowhere is this more evident than in the loading of your vehicle and the opportunity to include things which provide a sense of home.

Consider adding warmth and a sense of place to your RV by including some items for no practical reason other than that they make your RV "feel like home". Just what sorts of items those might be for you, I couldn't say. Perhaps some examples from our "home on wheels" will stimulate your thinking:

1. As mentioned previously, books are a big thing with us. We <u>never</u> leave on an RV outing with out having several times more books than we could possibly read.

2. Dave is a tea drinker and Kay likes a glass of wine before supper. Carefully packed in our cupboard are a Spode Tea Cup and Saucer along with a Riedel Crystal Wine Tumbler.

3. We both enjoy cooking. As you would expect, our kitchen is, compared to most other RV kitchens, intentionally over equipped.

4. We decided early in our RV travels we wanted our RV's contents to be functional *and* to serve as reminders of places we've been. Our "memory décor" includes a napkin holder from New Mexico, a "Cheeseburgers in Paradise" apron from Key West, a throw pillow from South Dakota, a lamp from North Carolina's Outer Banks, and a Cork Screw from the Napa Valley. I could continue on and on, but you get the idea.

The point is that our trailer is a reflection of us. It contains those things which make it seem personal, which define the space as ours, and which serve as reminders of the places we (Kay, Dave and "Big T") have gone together.

It is unlikely you will personalize your rental RV to the extent we have, over a span of many years, personalized our trailer. Our purpose here is to suggest you consider bringing a few things which are totally unnecessary and highly personal – preferably including at least a couple of things which are at least a bit eclectic. Bring something which will help you feel connected to your home on wheels. We suggest starting on this first trip with one thing each. On your next trip bring two.

Keep It (Not Too) Simple. Travel experts urge that we "keep it simple" . . . and for some types of travel that is appropriate, even necessary. In the case of RV travel, you have far more than a single suitcase worth of hauling space. You have much more room in which to exercise choice and flexibility. You can choose to "keep it simple". You can also decide not to.

Traveling by Preference. In deciding to go on an RV vacation you have made a choice to travel according to your own preferences. We suggest you load your unit in the same way. Put in those things which seem to you would add to your experience. You can always choose different stuff on your next trip.

Our suggested rule of thumb: when in doubt, toss it in. Toss it in, and from Day 1 maintain three lists in your RV: **First**, a list of things you wish you had with you and don't. **Second**, a list of things you have with you, but with no idea why. Your **third** list is one where you record those things you brought along and want to be certain you remember when you next travel by RV. With those three lists, the process of getting ready for your next trip will be greatly simplified.

PREPARE FOR BUGS

One final area before closing out this "What Should We Bring?" section: prepare for mosquitoes and other annoying insects.

Few things, blizzards and grossly inconsiderate neighbors are a couple of other possibilities, can spoil a mellow evening out-of-doors more quickly than an abundance of biting insects – each with a belief system which defines you as the evening's featured entrée. Not only are these little creatures highly annoying, some of them spread pretty nasty diseases.

Candles? Bug Spray? Screen Rooms? Special Clothing? If you have spent time out-of-doors in areas where such insects are a problem, you

---

$AVING$ TIP$

Buy Sunscreen and Insect Repellent Before You Leave Home. You can expect to pay double for the same stuff if you don't! When you are being eaten alive by mosquitoes, you won't be likely to spend much time looking for bargains.

---

have probably developed favored ways of dealing with them. If that describes your level of knowledge, just be sure to remember to bring along your favorite countermeasure: spray or candles or protective clothing or whatever.

If you don't know if insects are a problem at your destination, we suggest you find out and stock up on appropriate countermeasures before leaving home. Alternatively, you can wait until you arrive at your destination, assess the problem as you are eaten alive, and then pay inflated prices for whatever is the locally accepted repellent.

There are many who stress a lot over the whole packing process. They make endless lists and then make lists of the lists they are using – all in an attempt to insure they won't forget anything. We suggest a different approach: simply accept the fact that you will forget something. Also accept the fact the most things of significance can be purchased where you are going. If you must worry, focus on things which would be expensive, difficult or impossible to buy where you are going. (Prescription drugs and glasses are examples in the "difficult or impossible" group. Electronics, cameras and binoculars come to mind as expensive things to duplicate unnecessarily.)

In our experience, it is a given we will forget something. The fun part is seeing how long it takes us to figure out what it was. Usually, but not always, the things forgotten have been minor. We have been inconvenienced by our errors of omission, but never has a trip been ruined.

OK, you have finally reached a point where you know perhaps far more than you ever wanted to know about the process of renting an RV and of loading one for the road. **Now, it's time to get out and join "them that's doin'"**.

Part 3

Life on the Road

Rules of the Road
for RV Renters
(Classic Rules of Road-Tripping)

- Never pass up a chance to eat.

- Never pass up a chance for a nap.

- Expect to turn the wrong way at least some of the time.

- Allow time for unplanned discoveries.

- Never eat anything you _don't_ recognize.

- Never eat any place you _do_ recognize.

- Never bring stuff unless you know what it's for.

- You can always justify the purchase of more stuff.

- Always bring twice as much stuff as you need.

- Never leave a rest area without your spouse.

- Understand that first aid for hitch-itch always involves going somewhere.

- Don't start a trip on empty.

- Have some fun and don't forget why you left home.

Chapter Ten
Dealing with the Dealer – Part 2

The material in this chapter represents an interface, a junction point, between all you have done to get ready for your trip and actually getting on the road. Many of you, in your hurry to get going, will be inclined to skim over the activities suggested here and on the **Dealer Delivery Checklist** in **Appendix A**. At the time you accept delivery of your rental unit, there is greater opportunity for avoiding potential misunderstandings than at any single point in the RV rental process. We urge you to slow down. An extra hour or two with your dealer's representative now can have a major influence on the overall success of your trip.

You are finally ready to take delivery and get on with your vacation. Excitement is high. There will be a part of you wanting to skip all of this delivery stuff, to sign everything as fast as it is placed in front of you, and to get on the road. DON'T DO IT. Take time to understand how the systems in your RV work. Take time to be sure you and the dealer are in written agreement as to the physical condition of the unit you are accepting. Take time to be sure you understand how to operate all the systems in your new home on wheels. Take time to verify the presence of all agreed upon inclusions. Take time to confirm that paperwork and fees are as expected. Again, our advice is to slow down.

There are several phases to the delivery process and, while their order may vary, we stress the importance of each. Additionally, when you finally feel you are finished with all the preliminary stuff, you will want to make at least one final stop before you really get on the road. Let's get specific:

INSPECTION

Thoroughly go over your unit – top to bottom, inside and out – and look for damage. Look for anything that doesn't operate as it should. Pay particular attention to those items we have indicated on the **Dealer Delivery Checklist**.

Have the dealer make note of all blemishes and anything which doesn't operate exactly as it should.

The "Dealer Delivery Checklist" found in Appendix B has been designed to help you stay on track.

INVENTORY

Obtain from your dealer a list of everything which is supposed to be included with your unit and check to be sure it's all there. Include any vehicle or personal kits you are renting as extras. Pay attention to details – particularly in the kitchen – are the number of plates and glasses adequate? If pots, pans and cooking utensils are to be included, make sure they are there. Make sure any inventory discrepancies are corrected. Ask your dealer for any maps or guidebooks they have available.

$AVING$ TIP$

Avoid Last Minute, Impulse Purchases. Your dealer will most probably have an intriguing variety of gadgets and extras available for perusal and purchase. Consider only those you are positive you will find helpful. Ignore the others.

PRE-TRIP ORIENTATION

Your dealer should provide a pre-trip orientation. Prepare for that by reviewing the "systems overview" in Chapter 7 and reviewing the **Dealer Delivery Checklist** in **Appendix A**. Make sure you understand how to operate each of your unit's systems:

1. Learn how to fill the water and propane tanks.
2. And how to dump the holding tanks.

3. Find out how to operate the furnace and hot water heater, the generator and air conditioner.

4. How do you turn on the water pump and operate the shower?

5. How does the refrigerator work?

6. How do you open the windows, lock the doors, and operate the shades and blinds?

7. Is there a first aid kit?

8. Where do you find the spare and the jack and any emergency flares or triangles?

9. And, perhaps most important, where is the manual, where do you call if there is something you can't figure out, where do you call if you have a mechanical breakdown?

Make certain everything on the "Dealer Delivery Checklist" is covered.

PAPERWORK & PAYING

Since you have requested, received and reviewed your advance copies of all paperwork (you did do that, didn't you?), this phase of the delivery process should prove to be pretty straight forward. Get any last minute questions answered, be sure the forms you are being asked to sign are the same as the ones you were sent, and sign them.

$AVING$ TIP$

Understand Deposits. More specifically: be sure to find out up front <u>exactly</u> what will need to happen for your deposits to be refunded. As mentioned in the text, few dealers will be unreasonable about refunding your deposits . . . as long as you fulfill your end of the agreement.

NOTE: Before paying, confirm that the conditions for the return of your deposits are given in writing and that they are consistent with your previous understanding.

Some helpful hints for the "Paperwork & Paying" Phase:

1. Make sure you have with you any proof of insurance required by your rental company.

2. If there is any possibility the rental company will question your meeting their minimum driving age, be sure you can prove your age.

3. Bring a valid driver's license.

$AVING$ TIP$

Don't Buy Insurance You Don't Need. It is unlikely your existing insurance will extend to your RV rental. Most companies' coverage does not; however, yours might. Check with your insurance agent. Talk with your agent about what coverage they recommend for your RV rental vacation. It is a waste of money to over-insure or to be double insured, but it is not wise to go uninsured. Discuss appropriate coverage with your agent and then buy only what you need from your RV rental dealer.

A FAST STOP

One final thing before you hit the road: Unless you are taking your unit to your "sticks and bricks" home to load, you will want to stop at a store to stock up on consumables (paper products, cleaners, groceries). Don't just go wandering around in a strange town hoping to come across a store, ask your dealer where to find the most convenient one. And don't just go wandering around a strange store with no idea what you are looking for, bring a list. In the **Checklists Section – Appendix B** – we have included a list titled **"Preliminary Shopping List, Consumables"** to guide you during this initial stop. Of course you will want to modify the list to reflect your family's preferences.

Chapter Eleven
Movin' on Down the Road

Finally you are ready to hit the road!

When you started planning, this day seemed a vague point off somewhere in a far distant future. And now here it is! Months of thinking about your RV adventure are behind you. Anticipation and apprehension have peaked. Now it's time to get going and, in spite of all of your preparations, you find yourself facing a lot of unknowns.

$AVING$ TIP$

Go Easy on the Souvenirs. There is a limit to how many rubber alligators you really need. Admission tickets, a postcard, a few pictures, a pine cone from the mountains or a shell from the beach – all are excellent reminders of your first RV vacation.

This chapter deals with some common questions about traveling in an RV. The next chapter, **"Campground Considerations"**, addresses questions about setting up in, and living in, a campground.

RV DRIVING 101

Traveling by drivable RV brings literal truth to the old cliché, "getting there is half the fun". For many first time RVers, a logical extension of that thought might be, "getting there is half the fun . . . and 90% of the stress". The prospect of driving such a large, strange sort of vehicle for the first time can be a bit frightening.

Common concerns in the minds of those planning their first RV vacation cluster around the subject of driving: "How hard are they to drive?" "How do you see when you're backing up?" "How do you park one?" and so on and so on. Soothing answers to these, and similar questions, are found in doing. You will get comfortable with your home-on-wheels a lot sooner than you might now think.

Your dealer orientation will include guidelines and suggestions about how to actually drive your RV. This section isn't intended to replace your dealer orientation, but rather to supplement it by highlighting a few things you should be particularly conscious of. The point is simply to put forth a few tips you will find of value as you transition from driving the family car to driving the family house.

Taller, Wider, Longer, Heavier. Driving your RV is different than driving the family car – your RV is wider, significantly longer and taller . . . and a whole lot heavier. These differences require a driving process which is different. Different, but not difficult.

The skill set required to drive your RV is the same as required to drive the family car. The point is this: If you can drive a car, you can drive an RV. And if, as a driver of cars, you are a good, safe driver, there is no reason to think you will be other than a good, safe driver of your RV.

The central issue is this: **Remember Your Vehicle's Size**

When you first drive off in your new RV, you will be aware of the size of your vehicle . . . and that is a good thing. If there is a single key to driving an RV, it is to <u>always</u> remember you are driving a <u>really large vehicle</u>. ("Really large" is of course a comparative term. Your RV is really large *for a car*, but actually is pretty small *for a house*.) Vehicle size is an issue whenever you are moving – cornering, changing lanes, accelerating, or stopping. Size effects where you can stop for gas, for fast food, where you can park (remember to pay attention to height in addition to width and length).

It is easy to forget how large your vehicle is when you are comfortably cruising down an interstate highway . . . and that forgetting greatly increases the potential for problems in any situation. When you first start driving your new unit, no one needs to remind you that it is big. And that is a good thing. You are big, you are aware of it, and you are perhaps a bit nervous. Caution is required as you become accustomed to the size of your home on wheels. As you become comfortable with it.

The concern is this: As your comfort level increases, you may find yourself lapsing into old habits. You may find you are, <u>without really thinking about it</u>, driving your RV as if it were the family car. You may find yourself driving as if your vehicle were something less than huge. This is not a good time to slip into old driving habits.

Use Your Vehicle's Mirrors. Your mirrors, both sides, are of greater importance in your RV than in the family car. First, given that you are driving a unit significantly wider than that to which you are accustomed, your mirrors are a good way of seeing where you are in relation to the road. The striping on the road will be clearly visible in your mirrors and it is a fairly simple matter to stay oriented to the road relative to those stripes. <u>Caution: Don't become so attentive to the mirror's view of where you have been that you forget to pay attention to where you are going</u>.

A second value to your mirrors is in filling in the "blind spots" on each side of your vehicle. Given that what you are driving is a whole lot longer than the family car, it follows that your blind spots are also a whole lot larger. Your mirrors will help fill in these gaps, provide information about what is lurking alongside. When changing lanes, <u>always</u> signal, <u>always</u> check your mirrors and <u>always</u> have your co-pilot confirm your clearances.

And, I know this is redundant, no matter how comfortable you get driving your RV, always remember that you are behind the wheel of something taller, wider, longer and heavier than anything to which you are likely to be accustomed to driving. Keep size in mind, along with the *Three Rules of the Road RV Drivers*, and you'll be fine.

And what, you ask, are the **Three Rules of the Road for RV Drivers**? They are:

1. don't be in a hurry
2. Don't Be In A Hurry, and
3. DON'T BE IN A HURRY

More specifically:

1. Don't Be In A Hurry . . . To Get Going
2. Don't Be In A Hurry . . . To Get There (Speed)

3. Don't Be In A Hurry . . . To Get There (Driving Time)

It is worth a moment of your time for us to expand on those principals.

Don't Be In A Hurry . . . To Get Going

$AVING$ TIP$

Keep Tires Properly Inflated. Another fuel saver is to keep tire air pressures at the levels recommended by your dealer. Studies have shown that a single tire under inflated by 2 PSI can increase fuel consumption by 1%. It is scary to think about the impact it must have on gas mileage to drive a Class C Motorhome with 6 tires each under-inflated by 5 or 10 pounds!!

There is excitement as you begin your RV journey. Excitement to leave the dealers and get started on you new adventure. Excitement to leave the campground and get on the road. Excitement to get on with the day's planned sightseeing. In spite of the excitement, <u>don't be in a hurry to get going</u>.

No one knows your RV better than your dealer. As such, your dealer is your single best source of driving tips, tricks and techniques. There is an understandable degree of anxiousness, of excitement, while you are going through the dealer pre-trip orientation. This is arguably the single most important part of the RV rental process. Take your time. Make sure you understand everything your dealer is telling you. If there is anything you don't understand, take a few extra minutes to ask questions.

Each day, before starting out in your RV, take a moment to remember the advice you dealer gave you. Mentally review the lessons you have learned during your journey to this point. Only then, with guiding principals firmly in mind, should you head down the road.

Take Time to Set Up. Every time, before you take to the road, be sure your unit is set up properly. It only takes a few moments to check your tire pressure; to be sure your mirrors and seat are properly adjusted. Double check that loose items within the RV are properly stowed and that any potential distractions are under control. Wait until all passengers are buckled in.

Don't Be In A Hurry . . . To Get There (Speed)

$AVING$ TIP$

Avoid High Speeds. Depending on how much driving you do, fuel costs may be one of the most significant items in your RV rental vacation budget. One way of reducing those costs is to drive a bit slower. Driving at 75 mph will reduce your fuel consumption by around 15% when compared to what it would be if driving at 62 mph. Driving slower is also much safer and a lot less tiring.

Far too many RVers drive fast just because they can. There seems to be a misplaced sort of logic which says, "Heh, lookey here, this thing'll do 80!! We'll be there in no time." Just because your home on wheels is capable of going fast doesn't mean that it's a good idea. In fact, driving fast in an RV is an exceptionally bad idea.

Driving an RV requires your constant attention, your continuous awareness. Driving too fast shortens your time to think about what you are doing and decreases the time you have to react to things going on in the world around you. Anything which decreases your options is a bad idea. Excessive speed <u>always</u> reduces your options.

Stay in Your "Zone". Around, and particularly in front of, any moving vehicle is a zone which must remain clear for the driver to have time and space to respond to things as they happen around the vehicle. A large RV is less maneuverable and requires a far greater stopping distance than a standard sized car. As its driver, you need more space than you are used to . . . and the faster you go, the larger that "clear zone" needs to be.

Slow down and stay in your zone. The point in traveling by RV is to have a good time. Avoid doing anything which creates stressful or dangerous situations.

Don't Be In A Hurry . . . To Get There (Long Days)

Our final "don't be in a hurry" is to recommend that you not try to drive too many hours in a given day. Just how many hours are appropriate for you is something only you can determine. Simply remember that driving an RV is something which requires greater attention than driving down the same road in the family car. This greater focus, greater attention, translates into the fact that driving an RV is, other factors being equal, more tiring than cruising in the family van.

$AVING$ TIP$

Stop For a Roadside Picnic. The more meals you fix yourself, the more money you will save. It is that simple. As you travel in most tourist areas you will spot numerous, attractive road-side picnic areas. And in your home on wheels you should have all the fixings for a great picnic. You'll save money and have a great time with such impromptu little adventures. **NOTE:** Many picnic areas were designed before today's larger RVs. Don't pull into a picnic area, or anywhere else for that matter, without first seeing exactly how you will leave.

Take Time to Refresh. One factor which makes RV travel special is the ease with which you can pull off the road, into a rest area or picnic ground, for a really relaxing break. You have cold beverages (non-alcoholic if you are continuing your drive), a bathroom, even a bed to stretch out on.

In the event your plans require that you drive more than just a few hours on a given day, plan time for these breaks. You are going to a great deal of trouble and expense to travel with the comforts of home. Take time to enjoy them.

The Journey IS the Destination. The truth of this statement is seldom more obvious than when meandering about in an RV. Your vacation can be much more than the sum of your destinations. Like a "connect the dots" sort of picture, a full portrait of your RV vacation includes the passage between destinations. Allow a bit of extra time to enjoy the journey.

Buckle Up. Your rental RV will not only come with seat belts for each member of your party, but is likely to include a variety of secure seating options. There is clearly a great temptation to allow people to be up and moving about as you travel down the road. PLEASE DON'T!

Be aware that traveling in an RV without first buckling up exposes your passengers to hazards beyond those when traveling by passenger car. People up and moving about in an RV as it travels down the road face a risk of being thrown about during a sudden stop or emergency maneuver. Don't allow those traveling in your RV to take unnecessary risks. BE SAFE, BUCKLE UP!!!

THE FREEDOM OF THE ROAD

As you fall into the rhythm of RV travel, you will quickly discover why RVing is viewed by millions as something far beyond a transportation decision. To choose to travel by RV is to make a lifestyle choice and, while admittedly it is a choice not suitable to everyone, RV travel is clearly a vote in support of personal independence – a vote favoring the enhancement of life's journey.

Quick Stops. You will be free to stop where you want, for as long as you want and you will have your entire house with you when you do. Snacks and games. Changes of clothing and bathrooms. A spot for a quick nap. All travel with you.

Games & Entertainment. Your passengers can have a variety of entertainment options as you travel down the road in your house on wheels. In addition to travel standards, such as books, think about bringing along a board game or two (magnetic versions of popular games are particularly suitable). At a minimum, bring along a deck of cards. And, if you have arranged to have your unit appropriately equipped, you might even have a TV and a VCR available so that your passengers can enjoy a movie or two as you move from place to place.

Power to the People (Generator)

Your RV is likely to be equipped with a generator and, if so, you then have a source of 120-volt electricity even when you are not plugged into power at a campground. While traveling down the road the generator is what makes it possible to use your roof air conditioner – an important consideration in hot weather. The air conditioner in your vehicle's dash will not be adequate to cool the entire RV. Also, when stopped at a rest area, or in a shopping mall's parking lot, the generator will allow use of the air conditioner . . . plus your microwave, hairdryer, and most any appliance which requires conventional sorts of electricity.

$AVING$ TIP$

Buy Gas From Less Expensive Stations . . . and the least expensive stations may not be the major brands you are used to using. Pay attention to pricing. Filling the tank on a large Class A Motorhome, or even a moderate sized Class C, is a major event. Gas price research can be worth a few moments of your time. If you are traveling with a computer and are able to access the internet, check some gas cost web sites. These list stations with the lowest prices by city and zip code. While they may be of limited use in remote areas, they are generally worth at least a quick perusal. A couple of our favorites are www.gasbuddy.com and www.gaspricewatch.com.

Finally, and of most importance, **remember always to find pleasure in the journey**. Remain alert for new ways to enjoy the freedom provided by your choice of an RV vacation. You will find life on the road can be more fun than you ever thought possible. Life in a campground, the subject of our next chapter, is at least equally likely to exceed your expectations.

Chapter Twelve
Campground Considerations

Questions from new RVers tend to focus on getting from Point A to Point B. "How on earth do I drive one of these things?" Moving your RV from place to place is a central part RVing (which presumably is why we call them recreational *vehicles*); however, to focus only on the act of driving is to overlook many of the advantages of the lifestyle.

As the new RVer begins to actually live with their rental RV they also start to become aware of the advantages of the lifestyle. Here, for example, is one of the interesting things that happen: Your house will remain the same yet your backyard will change . . . perhaps daily. Let's take a look a just how you go about settling into a new neighborhood:

1st Rule of RVing - NEVER be Afraid to Ask.

You can choose to open your mouth, ask questions and admit you are new to this whole RVing thing, or you can keep your mouth shut and demonstrate your newness by your actions. Given these two options, even for guys who refuse to stop for directions, asking questions is the best, fastest (and often the only) way to figure out what it is you are wanting to know.

The point is that you, as one new to this RVing thing, shouldn't be shy about asking questions. Those of us who now feel at least a bit road worthy would love to show off a little by answering your questions. In fact, some of us, your authors for example, are not overly bright in the "how things work" arena. Your questions give us an opportunity to feel clever.

The Role of "Stupid Questions". It is said there are no such things as stupid questions. What nonsense! Of course there are! (We have asked most of them at least twice. And we have learned the most stupid of all are those which remain unasked.) The smart thing to do is to open your mouth and ask them. As indicated above, it is much appreciated when we RV veterans are presented with a question we can actually answer. Think of stupid questions as a gift you give to those of us capable of answering no other kind.

ARRIVING

The Entertainment Value of Newbies. OK, here comes a bit of pressure. In campgrounds throughout North American, and presumably elsewhere, a prime source of entertainment is the arrival of a new RVer – one who refuses to ask questions. And of all of those things a new RVer can do to entertain those already settled into the campground, nothing is more valued than backing into, or out of, your site.

Backing, Directing and the Value of Pull Thrus. Backing an RV is, for most of us, the most difficult part of learning to get around in one. In the first place your unit is really, really big and will grow by a factor of at least 2X as soon as you begin to back into a campsite. It is also a verifiable fact that campsites shrink dramatically, again by a factor of at least 2X, when approached by an RV. The backing process then demands that you then put a really, really large thing into a really, really small place. Oh yes, and if all that weren't difficult enough, you will need to do it without being able to see where you are going.

> **TIP:** If you are really uncomfortable with the idea of backing your RV, it is possible to get through your entire vacation without doing so. All that is required is that you think a bit ahead. First, and of greatest importance, <u>don't ever pull into any place without a clear idea of how you are going to get out.</u> And second, always ask for "pull through" sites when making your campground reservations. (A "pull-through" campsite is one which is open on both ends. The RVer pulls into the site driving forward and when the time comes to leave simply continues forward and exits the site on the other end.)

Most of you will find comfort in that you are not pulling a trailer. In trailer backing, the back of the trailer goes in the opposite direction of the back of the tow vehicle. You wind up trying to remember to turn to the left when what you really want to do is to go to the right – all as you try to put a really large trailer into a really small place (without seeing where you are going).

Actually, the difficulties in backing drivable RVs are a bit overstated – particularly for those of you with a moderate size Class C or one of the even smaller Class Bs. Having said that, we also understand that backing is a major concern for many.

You will get along fine if you remember just a few concepts:

1. You will not be able to see much about where you are going. Always have someone outside of your vehicle to direct you.

2. The person doing the directing must remain in sight of the driver at all times. The person doing the directing must remember that if they can't see the driver, either directly or in a rear view mirror, the driver can't see them.

3. The person directing must give directions which are both clear and simple. Anything beyond "Turn Left", "Turn Right", "Come On Back" and "Stop" are too subjective to be of value to the driver.

4. Drivers should not only move slowly, but should never move at all without a clear idea of where they are relative to where they are trying to go.

5. The single best piece of advice we can give about backing is this: Any time your situation is anything other than perfectly clear, get out and take a look.

6. Finally, remember that when backing the best maneuver is often to pull forward with the intention of changing your angle of approach.

The Importance of Being Level. One other factor in the parking process: There are a variety of reasons why it is important to have your RV at least somewhat level when stopping for an extended period. In a severely out of level RV walking can be interesting, sleeping impossible, and your refrigerator may not work.

Fortunately, most spaces in commercial/private RV parks are adequately level for your purposes. Spaces in state and federal campgrounds vary widely as to their suitability for RVs. You will find some which are of adequate size and are perfectly level. Others will be so far out of level that there will be no possibility of making them work.

You will find, within reason, you can "feel" whether your unit is level or not. As a double check, most RVers carry a level of one sort or another with them. (Some, but not all, rental RVs have levels attached.)

How to Get Level. In most cases if you find your unit is only slightly out of level, simply moving forward or backward a bit will provide adequate adjustment. With sites which are moderately sloping, placing blocks under the tires on the low side of your unit is perhaps the simplest way to bring your unit to level. (A few rental RVs will have leveling systems built in. The majority will not.) When severely out of level, the best bet is to request that you be assigned a different site. The point is to be acceptably level before getting settled into your new surroundings.

One final thought before you get too comfortable in your new neighborhood: Do you need propane? Butter? Eggs? Beer? From personal experience we assure you it is frustrating to be stopped for the day, settled into your campsite for the evening, and then recognize you are out of something critical. It seems to be a fact of RV life that you will at least once experience the need to disconnect everything, put everything away, and drive to the store. Better to remember needed stuff before you get too relaxed.

Recommending the Minimalist

When setting up in a new campground, take a minimalist approach. Don't drag out everything in the RV just because it is there. Don't hook up everything just because you remember how.

Do As Little as Possible. If you need a rule of thumb for setting up your RV on arrival at a new campground, or upon your return to the previous night's site following a day's outing, it would be this: do as little as possible. Don't hook it up, turn it on, or drag it out unless you believe you will have use for it before time to move on.

Setting Up. Those who RV soon develop their own style, their own system, for setting up at a new campsite. You will quickly develop a routine which suits you. While you are figuring out your own way of doing things, here are a few tips gleaned from the hundreds of nights we have spent on the road:

Water, Electric & Wait. First, decide who is in charge of the inside and who is going to do the outside stuff. In our travels, Dave does the outside set up and Kay the inside. You will find if you don't divide up the territory you will spend a lot of time bumping into each other and generally not getting things done.

Our routines vary a bit with the length of our planned stay. On a simple overnight stop, we connect to electricity and water. That's all there is to it. Plug it in, connect the water hose, and then wait to see if anything else is needed. By way of example, it makes no sense to set up the charcoal grill until you plan to use it. The same is true of the rest of the process.

Act on an "As Needed" Basis. This is not rocket science, simply common sense. Everything you get out, hook up or turn on will need to be put away, disconnected or turned off when it is time to move on. <u>And</u> you are living in a small place compared to your sticks and bricks home; it is easy to get it junked-up and cluttered.

> **TIP: <u>Always Know What County You Are In</u>**. Severe weather can be frightening in general and more so when in an RV in a strange area. Severe weather alerts are announced most frequently by county – a pretty meaningless bit of information to an outsider with not the slightest idea what county they are in. Both the Woodall's and the Trailer Life Directories give the county in which each campground is located at the very first part of their listings.

SETTLING IN

Settling in upon arrival at a new campground is a simple process. Don't needlessly complicate it.

There are those who arrive at each new campsite with a great deal of drama. We hear a startling amount of noise – much yelling and banging things together – and see a lot of interesting arm waving and scurrying about. These people tend to drag everything out – presumably so they can put most of it away again – and do not seem well served by their approach.

In contrast our arrival is sedentary. We simply do the minimum, then pause to see what develops.

We View Arrival as a Process, an event which continues until we begin preparations for leaving. Beyond the basics, we have no predetermined routine. Setup is a gradual procedure which takes place as needs arise. The longer we stay in one place, the more settled in we become.

Given our way of doing things, an "**Arrival Checklist**" is pointless. You could of course use such a list if you'd like. (One is included in our workbook "***Travel Planning for RV Renters***").

Household "Short Cycle". Inside our unit, we operate on what we call a "Short Cycle" – meaning we only get out those things we actually need and we put things away when we are not actively using them. This is not because we're a couple of compulsives who must always have things perfect – far from it! It is just that, compared to the smallest sticks and bricks home, an RV is a really small living space. Without a bit of discipline, you will be shocked at how quickly your space will become totally cluttered.

In an RV some routine of clutter control is essential. Also there is this: Nearly everything you get out will need to be put away before you can head out the next morning anyway, so why not cut down on the departure scramble and put things away as you go?

A Place for Everything. As you move into your home on wheels, you will tend to shove things into whatever space they will fit. That is just the way of it. Living with an RV longer term leads to a "place for everything" mentality. You will soon find you have a sort of organizational system for everything in your rental RV. Actually, "system" is probably too strong of a word, but you will have places where you generally put things.

Don't worry about it (though you should take some extra care to pack any breakables securely). Everything will still find its place. You will not always be able to immediately recall precisely where that spot might have been; however, there are a limited number of places for things to hide in an RV. Though stuff may have a tendency to become "temporarily unavailable" (as opposed to actually lost), it is difficult to permanently misplace anything in an RV.

$AVING$ TIP$

Take Advantage of Campground Recreational Offerings. Plan some "do-nothing" time. Stay in the same campground for an extra night and spend a day just hanging out. Lay around the pool. Read a book. Fix a special meal. Enjoy a sunset. You'll find some of your best vacation memories in those times when you did absolutely nothing – as in, *"We woke up in the morning with absolutely nothing to do and went to bed that evening having only accomplished about half of it."*

LIVING THE LIFE

Think Outside the Box. TV is a thing difficult to work out with most rental RVs. Most do not come with a TV. Many do not have antennas or provisions for connecting to cable. I have never seen a fleet rental unit with a satellite dish. If TV is something you feel you simply can't do without, talk to your rental dealer and see what you can work out. We are not saying that TV in a rental RV is impossible, simply that it is often more trouble than it is worth. You will find in many vacation areas, reception is limited at best.

A Rental Car? Your drivable RV can be less than an ideal vehicle for cruising around congested tourist areas. Parking is generally provided for RVs, but can sometimes be a problem. Driving a large, unfamiliar vehicle in high density tourist traffic is not the most pleasant of experiences. If your plans include staying in one area – one base camp – for a number of days, you might want to explore the idea of getting a rental car. Many campgrounds can make arrangements for you.

A rental car will take some of the stress out of your daily driving. It will allow you to avoid the need of constantly hooking up and unhooking, getting things out only to immediately put them away. In short, it will enable you to settle into your RV as your vacation home.

Living the Life. In most campgrounds and RV parks, evenings are a wonderfully laid back sort of time. People are relaxed, friendly and just generally enjoying the experience of being precisely where they are.

Evenings are a favorite time and what we've come to think of as our evening "walk-about" is a favorite activity. As you might assume, the evening walk-about is simply wandering around a campground in a delightfully unfocused, nonspecific sort of way. We stroll along – no power walking allowed – observing the variety of rigs, checking out license plates and stopping to visit now and then.

An interest in travel and a shared lifestyle provide common ground, a bridge across social and economic differences, and confirm the general truth that RVers are a friendly and outgoing group. We usually learn a bit – RVers love to talk about their "homes on wheels" and their activities. We find out where people have been, where they are going. We discuss our rigs, and share both tips and experiences. These things are part of what makes an evening in an RV park special. If you are new, and if our paths cross, know that there is little we like more than easing the learning curve of those new to our lifestyle.

Campground Notes. For us, an additional purpose of the evening walk-about is to check out the campground in more detail. Blank index cards and a pen are carried to jot down the numbers of any sites we find particularly desirable or which we want to make a special note to avoid on future visits. When we return to our trailer, we transfer our notes to one of our **"Campground Scouting Reports"** (see **Appendix B**). Having made this a practice for a number of years, we have reference notes on hundreds of campgrounds – both those we view positively and those with which we were less than pleased.

Staying Connected. There are a variety of ways in which RVers stay in touch with friends and relatives while on the road. There are of course the traditional postcards and letters home, but there are a lot of other possibilities:

Virtually all commercial campgrounds have **pay phones**. Bring a calling card with you and you'll find the process of calling home to be a simple, though not always convenient, one.

It seems nearly everyone today has a **cell phone.** We are often asked how well cell phones work while RVing. It is too general of a question to answer. It depends on who your service provider is and on their coverage in the area to which you are traveling. Some of the most desirable destination campgrounds are found off of the beaten path – and out of range of the nearest cell towers. We prefer to travel in comparatively remote areas and have found our phones work in our base camp maybe half of the time. We frequently adjust our sightseeing routines to allow time for calling wherever and whenever we find a strong enough signal.

Another popular option for staying in touch is e-mail. We find that nearly all campgrounds in our recent experience have places where we can plug in our lap top to send and receive e-mail (you will of course need either a local access number or an 800 number for your dial-up service). At the time of this writing, late 2005, we are finding great numbers of campgrounds, truck stops and coffee shops have installed WiFi Hotspots and literally thousands more will be set up in the coming months. These installations can enable the RVer traveling with a lap top to sit in their home on wheels and be connected to the entire world.

THE TRIP DIARY

Highly recommended is the practice of maintaining some sort of trip diary or RV Journal – any form of making a systematic record of things you learn and experience on your journeys. Plan to start this practice at the beginning of your RV adventure. If you later decide it is a waste of time, you can always throw it away. Retrieving information which you failed to record is more difficult.

We are not recommending a rambling sort of narrative journal, though many keep such a record. Our point is that you implement some sort of systematic way of jotting down details, lessons, and experiences which might be lost over time. As your journeys and experiences accumulate over the years, your journal will become a valuable source of planning reminders, a critical aid in planning future travels.

Deciding what form your journal takes and specifically what you record in it are both personal and important. Exact details as to form and content are not nearly as important as the consistent recording of information.

You may choose a spiral notebook, a large or a small blank journal, and may be comfortable with either lined or unlined pages. Many like the "prompting" aspect of our fill-in-the-blank form **"Today's RV Adventures"**. This form is included in our workbook **"Travel Planning for RV Renters"** and is also available as a separate **"RV Adventure Journal"**. Both are can be ordered at: www.RVRentalGuide.com.

We don't recommend any of the commercially available generic "travel journals". Much of their format is not appropriate to your RV adventure. Such journals are designed for a different type of travel and include space for the recording of information not applicable to the RV experience. They also fail to include space for recording stuff we RVers find important.

We don't claim that the preformatted pages offered in any travel journal, including ours, are strictly necessary. You might get along fine with a simple spiral notebook. The downside of using a blank notebook is, in the absence of the "fill in the blank" sort of prompting, you will forget to record something important. As a proportion of your total trip expense the cost of a travel journal is pretty minor. Assuming of course that you use it, its format might remind you to note an important detail which could otherwise be lost.

The Practice of Journal Keeping. Journal keeping is a pretty personal sort of thing. To give you some ideas as to form, method, and supplies you might want to bring along, we include here a bit of information from Dave about the way he keeps our journal:

"Journal entries are made first thing in the morning (evenings don't work for me because my mind turns to mush at around 7:00 P.M.) and each entry covers the previous day. I like using a roller-ball type of pen and use a different

color on each trip – a small point, but with a journal now totaling hundreds of pages the changing colors makes it easier to find the specific entries for a particular outing.

"Our entries include: the date, where we are, what campground we are staying in, and specifically what space we are in. We record our impressions of both the campground generally and of our space specifically – good and bad. A habit we have developed over the years is that of an evening "walk about". During that time of roaming around the campground we make note of both spaces which seem particularly desirable and of places we'd like to avoid on future trips. Many campgrounds, both public and private, allow you to reserve specific sites, though there are notable exceptions – the California State Park System being one which comes to mind.

"If the previous day has been one of travel, the entry includes how far we drove, how long it took and anything significant about our route. We also record daily temperatures – highs and lows – and note any particularly good or bad weather. On those days we eat out, if we have a particularly memorable meal (memorable in either a good or a bad sense of the word), we record where and what we ate. We also make very brief notes about where we went and what we did during the previous day. That's pretty much it."

We have learned it is important to keep our entries short and to the point. Longer, more rambling entries create, for us at least, two problems. First, going back to find a specific bit of information is more difficult. Second, the longer and more complex the entry, the less likely we are to do it at all.

We know we are repeating ourselves here, but we have found this to be an important practice: We allow time to check out other campgrounds in every area we visit – for our own future reference and to enable us to offer informed suggestions to others visiting the area. We record our general impressions of those other campgrounds and we make note of the most desirable sites. Our campground notes are maintained separately from our RV Journal, though we couldn't really say just why that is. We use our **"Campground Scouting Report"** (included in Appendix B), fill out a separate one for each campground and file them by state, alphabetically by campground name, in a three-ring binder.

MOVING ON

At some point, the time to move on arrives. The process doesn't vary significantly whether you are leaving in your RV for a day's site seeing or leaving to move on to another campground hundreds of miles down the road.

It isn't a particularly difficult process. The arrival process is a sort of self-regulating one – things you fail to hook up properly bring themselves to your attention by not working. Preparing to depart is a bit more memory dependent, but no more complex. Preparing to leave is basically a matter of remembering what you did when you arrived and undoing it.

Inside & Out. Because we have no specific system/routine governing what we drag out and hook up when we arrive, it is easy to forget what we have done as the time comes to depart. Given our approach to the arrival process, "**Departure Checklists**" are essential. We have one for inside preparations and a separate one for outside. Copies of each are included in **Appendix B**. We urge you to use **Departure Checklists** – ours or one of your own design – every time you prepare to leave a campsite, NO EXCEPTIONS. As you scurry around getting ready to leave, steps in the departure process can be easily forgotten without some sort of list.

In our experience, preparing to leave a campground presents far greater potential for error than does arrival. We find it tempting to skip our checklists when we've only made a brief, one night stop; however, we have also found those occasions to be the ones where we are most likely to make mistakes.

Two people trying simultaneously to get the same part of the same RV ready for the road will spend a lot of time in one another's way. You will find it most efficient if, as you did on arrival, one of you to prepares the inside for travel while the other works outside disconnecting and putting things away.

You will find that many of the items on our checklists do not apply to your RV and that other items apply only part of the time. Ignore or draw lines through those parts which don't apply. If you decide to move into the RV life style on a more consistent basis, these lists will provide a good starting point for the development of your own.

A final departure tip: After you have pulled out of your spot, at least one of you should do a quick, final check for things that you may have overlooked. Check under the picnic table, look for things which may have been under your unit before you pulled out. Don't take a lot of time with this step, but don't skip it either. Finding something of importance which was about to be left behind can save you a lot of future aggravation.

For most of you, you will have just started to get into the rhythm of the RV lifestyle when the time comes to bring your experiment to an end. **How to prepare for the return of your unit to the dealer, how to prepare for the return of yourself to "real" life, and where do you go from here?** These are the questions we deal with in the next chapter.

Chapter Thirteen
And Then We Were Done
A Gentle Conclusion

At some point, unless you decide to join the over one million Americans who have made RV living their fulltime lifestyle, your RV adventure will end. For many of you it will be only the end of "Act 1" in your life as an RVer. All of you will go through the steps of returning your rental unit to your dealer . . . and of deciding what to do next.

DEALING WITH THE DEALER – PART III

Understand Dealer Requirements - In Advance!! Your dealer's requirements for the return of the rental unit tend to be both reasonable and expected. We previously suggested that, before taking delivery of your unit, you double check that you understand what the requirements are for its return and the refund of your deposit(s). Generally, dealer expectations are pretty straight forward – they want the unit returned in the same condition it was at the time you took delivery. Included in **Appendix B** is a **"Dealer Return Checklist"** to provide some guidance in preparing your unit.

> **A Couple of Reminders:** These points were highlighted in Chapter 10. For the benefit of those of you not reading this book in order (which we suspect is a significant majority) we repeat them here:
>
> 1. Find out when taking delivery if the dealer has an area where you can clean your unit immediately prior to its return. Find out if you can dump your holding tanks there.
>
> 2. Be sure you understand up front the requirements for the return of your deposit(s). Few dealers are unreasonable about the return of deposits; however, the opportunity for avoiding misunderstandings is at the time of delivery, not at the end of your journey.

Understand Dealer Requirements - In Advance!! Your dealer's requirements for the return of the rental unit tend to be both reasonable and expected. We previously suggested that, before taking delivery of your unit, you double check that you understand what the requirements are for its return and the refund of your deposit(s). Generally, dealer expectations are pretty straight forward – they want the unit returned in the same condition it was at the time you took delivery. Included in **Appendix B** is a **"Dealer Return Checklist"** to provide some guidance in preparing your unit.

Cleaning. You will be expected to return the unit in clean, re-rentable condition. Floors, counter tops, bathroom, windows – all will need to be in pretty much the same condition as when you rented the unit. The holding tanks were empty when you accepted delivery of the unit; they will need to be empty when you bring it back.

Refueling. You probably took delivery of your unit with a full tank of gas and with a full propane tank. This isn't rocket science here . . . you will be expected to return your unit with these tanks as when you took delivery – full.

Deposits. You will have been charged a deposit, probably several, when you took delivery. A deposit for cleaning, for fuel, for mileage and so on. Review the conditions for return of these deposits before turning your unit back to the dealer and be sure you have done your part.

Personal Property Triple Check. Finally, when you are sure everything which should be full is, everything cleanable has been cleaned, and you have emptied everything it is appropriate to empty, do a double check, a triple check, to be sure you've removed all of your personal property. Look in, under and behind <u>everything</u> and then do it again.

After you are sure you have removed the last of your personal property, it is time to turn your unit back to the dealer and for you to move on.

A BRIEF TRANSITION

You are neither here nor there. You have returned your rental unit and, for the moment at least, are no longer an RVer. You have not yet returned to your sticks and bricks place of residence.

This Is The Time Between Times . . . a brief interlude before returning to daily routines and after your adventure. It is a good time to reflect. To evaluate. How you choose to follow-up your RV adventure will depend on how you feel about it and you may need a bit of time and bit of distance from that experience to really know how you feel.

You will have been changed by your travels. If in no other obvious way, you will at least know more about the RV lifestyle and about how you feel about it. So what do you do next? The question doesn't require an answer in the form of a long term commitment. It directs you only to look towards the next logical step.

Some of you will find the lifestyle particularly suits you. If you find yourself in this group, it might make sense to explore the possibility of buying some sort of RV for your own use. You needn't, by the way, feel any need to run out and buy the "perfect" RV. In reality there probably isn't a perfect RV. Even if there were, you don't yet know enough about your wants, needs, desires and preferences to know precisely what that perfect unit might be.

At the other end of the scale, there will be a few of you who find you really don't like the RV way of doing things. Suffice it to say that we won't be likely to run into one another at a campground any time in the foreseeable . . . and that's also OK. The important thing is that you gave it a chance and because you did you can now add the experience to your "Been there done that" list and move on.

There is a third group of you who find themselves neither infected by the RV bug nor ready to exclude the possibility of another RV vacation in the future. Yours is a group which is best served by giving the entire RV experience a bit of incubation time. Your next step, perhaps another RV rental vacation and perhaps not, will be much clearer in a month or two or six.

BACK TO THE "REAL WORLD"

Decompressing - A Return "Home". We have found a variety of responses within ourselves as we have, over many years, returned to various sticks and bricks houses following RV trips which now number beyond recollection. We have noticed tendencies, a pattern in our reactions. Perhaps in time you will discover similar directions in you feelings?

Joy . . . particularly in the early stages of RV travel, many find a sense of joy, of freedom, upon returning. The family car will seem unexpectedly small and maneuverable. Your sticks and bricks house, contrasted to the RV in which you have spent the past week or two, will be far more spacious than you remembered.

and Sadness. As you adjust to the RV lifestyle, you may find your reactions at the end of a trip shifting. We now walk into our sticks and bricks house and see little but work undone – weeds to get rid of, mail to sort, bills to pay, household repairs too long put off. We know that every morning, until our next trip, we will wake up, look out the window and see the same yard.

There is a general feeling we have increased our living space – and the amount of stuff we are surrounded by – relative to our RV existence. We also have a heightened understanding of the price we are paying for our sticks and bricks existence. We have traded freedom for the opportunity to stay home and take care of our stuff. We find increasing inclination to let go of the stuff, return to the road, and take care of ourselves.

A JOURNEY THAT NEVER ENDS

For some of us the only solution short of selling all and going full timing – actually a pretty attractive option in the big picture – is to create a way of thinking in which the journey never ends. What many see as the end of one trip, we have learned to view as the beginning of the next.

"Hitch Itch". Don't be surprised to find similar feelings within yourself. Don't be surprised if one day as you are driving to work, you see an RV on the road and find you are curious where they are headed, find yourself wondering how long they've been on the road, find yourself wishing you were somewhere, out there, also.

When you find yourself with these feelings, and when they reach an intensity which is hard to ignore, then you'll know you too are a victim of "hitch-itch". (You can't say we didn't warn you.) Early on in this work we talked about the risks of hitch-itch . . . and we explained that all known cures are both temporary and involve going somewhere.

The Planning Begins. In our lives we have adopted a practice of always being involved with a trip. When not actually traveling, we are <u>always</u> at some point in the process of planning our next outing. Many of our trips, outlined in exquisite detail, only take place on paper. For a variety of reasons we are often unable to go. The planning process is not even a temporary cure for hitch-itch, but it is a pleasant distraction.

You are now a seasoned RVer. You know infinitely more than when you started on this journey. You have collected some memories, maybe a bit of stuff, and have formed some opinions. Among those this book has helped introduce to the RVing lifestyle are a few who have caught a severe case of hitch-itch and a portion of those will spend the rest of their lives wandering from place to place in an RV. We feel pretty good knowing that.

In our final few chapters we cover some specific RV rental situations which will not be applicable to all of you. You will find expanded information about fly/drive RV rental vacations, information about traveling with pets, and a brief discussion about RVing for those with special needs.

Part 4

Special
Considerations

Chapter Fourteen
Special Considerations
Fly/Drive RV Rentals

There are three areas of significant difference in the fly/drive RV rental vacation as compared to a vacation where you rent closer to home. There are some additional things to think about in selecting a dealer, some added challenges in selecting your rental unit, and a diminished opportunity to bring "stuff" from home. Let's take a look at these areas:

DEALER CONSIDERATIONS

Earlier in this book, specifically in Chapter 5, we discussed dealer selection. Here we point out that for the fly/drive RVer it is necessary for you to make a decision which is arguably more important and to do so with less information.

The fly/drive RV renter is at the mercy of the dealer. You will fly to a distant location to pickup a unit from a rental dealer you have never actually visited. At that point, should you find something which is not acceptable and/or which has been misrepresented, you have few options. You are committed. You are stuck.

The fly/drive situation is one in which you make a high level of commitment and do so with a limited amount of information. You have neither the opportunity to preview the dealer's inventory nor a chance to meet your dealer face-to-face.

The risks in dealer and unit selection are greater in a fly/drive vacation. So are the rewards in traveling to a distant, and presumably more exotic, destination. Be aware of the additional challenges in arranging this type of trip. Be aware, but don't stress over it. Here are some specific things you can do to increase your chances of having a wonderful vacation:

Consideration Number 1 – Chain or Local Independent? For the fly/drive vacationer, the national chains of RV rental dealers may have a significant advantage over the local independent. This is true in at least two perspectives:

1. In the absence of a personal recommendation from a trusted source, the only thing you have to go on is dealer reputation. It is far easier to get a handle on dealer reputation when checking out large companies with multiple outlets than when trying to get a feel for the reliability of a local mom and pop operation. This isn't to say there is anything wrong with the smaller outfits, only to point out that it's more difficult to get reliable information at a distance.

2. Additionally, any company which has outlets both close to you and where you are traveling presents an opportunity to preview units which are at least similar to those you are thinking of renting. Previewing will give you a feel as to general suitability and an indication of maintenance standards. There is no guarantee the maintenance standards at the outlet where you plan to rent will be exactly the same as at the outlet where you are previewing, but the odds are they will be similar.

Paperwork, Paperwork. Assuming you don't plan to show up for delivery of your rental unit and passively sign everything placed in front of you – without question, perhaps even without reading – you should ask your distant dealer for copies in advance of everything you will be asked to sign. Repeat and reemphasize that you want copies of <u>everything</u> and <u>in advance</u> of your scheduled arrival. Should you find your selected dealer hesitant, double-talking, or actually refusing to provide you the requested paperwork, be prepared to reevaluate your choice.

Read all of your paperwork in advance (and preferably not just on the plane while on the way to pickup your rental unit). Study with highlighter in hand

and mark any areas of question or concern. Include both those clauses you don't understand and those you do understand and don't like.

Don't wait until you arrive to pickup your unit to get answers to your questions or to put forth objections to what you find in your paperwork. The greater your level of commitment, the lower your negotiating leverage. (Not that the dealer is likely to agree to rework their paperwork for your benefit anyway, it is just that your ability to negotiate will drop from negligible to none if you wait until the last minute.)

As we stated in Chapter 5, the paperwork will be slanted for the benefit of the party with the highest investment in the transaction – which is of course the dealer. Perhaps that is as it should be. The point here is the importance of your understanding your rights, and your lack of rights, in the transaction prior to your scheduled pickup. In the event the paperwork contains a clause which you just cannot accept, it is important you discover that while you still have an opportunity to change your plans.

Dealer Pickup At Airport? Find out if your dealer will pick you up at the airport. If not, find out what form of transportation your dealer recommends.

Again, the point here is to ask these questions before you make a final commitment to a rental dealer. We don't recommend you consider this point a major one in your dealer selection process. On the other hand, if you have two dealers which seem otherwise comparable it makes sense to go with the one who makes the process the most convenient for you.

Another area to discuss with your dealer before committing: Will the arrival time of your flight allow you to get to the dealers during their normal business hours? If not, what do you plan to do about it?

The objective here, as in so much we have talked about in these pages, is to eliminate as many surprises as possible. If you have not figured out how to get from the airport to the dealers, if you are arriving when the dealer is closed and if you begin the process of dealing with either of these situations at the last moment, you will have needlessly raised the opening stress level of your vacation.

UNIT SELECTION

Selection of the rental unit most likely to provide an outstanding vacation experience hinges on two unrelated areas: Is the general layout of the unit comfortable? (Is the size appropriate, the floor plan workable – does it "feel right"?) And, has the unit been adequately maintained? (Is the living space clean and not unduly worn? How likely are there to be mechanical problems?)

The Importance of Condition. In our interviews as we prepared to write this book, the single most common area of dissatisfaction heard from others about their rental RV experiences related to the condition of their units. We heard complaints about both cosmetic condition and mechanical condition.

Mechanical condition is a difficult thing to prejudge excepting that there is perhaps a correlation between cosmetic condition and mechanical condition. The assumption is that a unit which has been poorly maintained cosmetically is likely to have also been poorly maintained mechanically. Maintenance standards are highly important and are at best difficult to judge in units which are not available for inspection. There are a couple of things you can do:

1. You may find a national chain with outlets both in your general home base area and in your destination. Simply go to the local outlet with an eye towards judging the condition of the distant units. It is an unwarranted leap of logic to assume the condition of the distant units is demonstrated by those you see locally. On the other hand, it is at least an indication.

2. In the absence of a local representative, find out the average age of units in the fleet at the outlet where you intend to rent. Age is not an absolute indicator of condition; however, older, higher mileage units will tend to be in worse cosmetic condition and more likely to have mechanical problems than their newer counterparts.

Finally, call the destination outlet. Talk with their representative about their cosmetic and mechanical maintenance standards. You can't expect the representative to admit their outfit employs a bunch of slobs (even if that is the case); however, the representative's comments might give you a feel as to the importance they place on maintenance issues.

Model Selection. An opportunity to locally preview units similar to the model you are thinking of renting increases the odds you will select a unit which passes your "live in" test. We have reviewed some things you can do to increase the odds of finding a unit which is adequately maintained, but what about simply finding a unit that "feels right"?

For those without extensive time spent actually living in RVs, a group which includes a sizable portion of RV renters, visualizing the suitability of a specific RV based on a small floor plan and perhaps a few pictures is nearly impossible. Yet that would seem to be the only basic option when your selected unit is not available for previewing.

To judge the suitability of a specific size/type/floor plan/model of RV with a reasonable degree of competence requires, as we discussed in Chapter 4, at least a little time actually in a unit which is at least very similar to the one you intend to rent. Time to sit back, look around, and ask, "Could I be comfortable living in here for a week or two?" Time to see if the unit "feels right".

When your plans involve the fly/drive approach to your RV vacation there are three common ways to approach the "sit and feel" test:

1. If working with a national chain (we keep coming back to that factor) with an outlet both in your general area and in the area to which you are traveling, you are likely to find similar models at both locations. In that case, it is a simple matter of going to your local outlet to check out the models you are considering.

2. In the absence of a similar local outlet, your next best bet becomes the RV Show. See if there is one coming up in your area. If so, go there and check out units in varying sizes and price ranges. (Any resemblance between your rental unit and the $1,000,000 motor home at the show will be pretty superficial.) For those new to the RV lifestyle, an RV show can provide the greatest exposure in the least amount of time.

3. Find out the brand(s) carried by the fly/drive outlets you are considering. Then check, probably on the manufacturer's web site, to see if you have a local sales outlet for that brand. If so, go there and check them out. Know that your rental unit will be pretty much lacking the bells and whistles seen on the units available for purchase, but the basics will be the same.

As you mull over the possibilities, remember storage isn't of as much importance in a rental unit as in a unit you are planning to purchase. It just doesn't require that much storage to put away a suitcase full of clothes and a less than minimal amount of kitchen stuff.

SOME COMMENTS ABOUT "STUFF"

Having reviewed the material in Chapters 8 and 9, you are aware that most of the stuff you need to actually live in your RV won't be included in your basic rental fee. It may not make sense, but that is the way things are.

> ## $AVING$ TIP$
>
> **Take Advantage of Dealer's Equipment Rentals**. Given the limited options available for fly/drive RV renters, it will be far cheaper to rent "kitchen kits" and "personal kits" from your dealer than to attempt to go out and buy the same stuff. For those who already have items which are the equivalent of those in the dealer's kits, the least costly option of all is, whenever possible, to outfit the RV with those things which are already owned.

As one flying to your point of rental, you will almost always be best off to rent "personal kits" and a "vehicle kit" from your dealer (the names for these "kits" will vary somewhat). The point here is to know in advance *exactly* what is (and what isn't) included in these kits and *exactly* what they cost.

You could travel to your destination with a duffel bag full of sleeping bags, bedding and towels. You could also stop somewhere and purchase most of the items in a standard dealer's vehicle kit. You could do those things and maybe even save a few dollars. As you weigh your options, most of you will decide the extra cost of renting these items from you dealer is worth it for the added convenience.

A caveat about stuff. The fly/drive vacationer has a far different set of issues surrounding the nature and amount of personal stuff than the vacationer renting locally with plans to simply pull the vehicle into their home driveway and throw stuff in until it is full.

First, know the stuff "needed" *will* exceed your airline's luggage restrictions. Early in this work, we pointed out that a significant advantage to an RV vacation is the capacity to bring major amounts of personal stuff. For the fly/drive vacationer, the ability to carry lots of stuff in an RV is limited by the amount of stuff you can bring on a commercial airline.

Start figuring out how you are going to approach the stuff situation by recognizing that, while you can bring a lot on an airplane, you will not be able to bring as much as you might like. The limiting "stuff factor" is your airline's luggage restrictions. While you can choose to exceed your baggage allowance, in most cases the costs in doing so make this an unwise option. Recognize that you can only bring a portion of what you might otherwise like to have along. Then decide how you are going to deal with your shortage. Here are some options for your consideration:

1. **They Sell Stuff There.** The first point is that almost anything you might want, and yet be unable to bring on the plane for whatever reason, will be available for purchase where you are going.

2. **Know Your Airline's Rules.** Your first step is to find out specifically what the luggage allowance is on the airline on which you will be flying. At the time of this writing, it seems that most airlines are very similar, if not identical, in their allowances.

   50# x 4 = 200 Pounds!! Plus Carryons!!! Given common airline baggage allowances, and the limited and casual nature of RV wardrobe requirements, you have the opportunity to bring really a significant amount of stuff with you. Assuming a traveling party of two, each with an allowance of 2 bags of 50 pounds each, you can potentially bring 200 pounds of stuff! Plus a carryon each. While that might leave you a bit limited on the amount of cast iron cookware you'll bring, the potential is for a bunch of stuff.

On the subject of luggage, **give thought to what you plan to do with your empty suitcases**. A party of two with maxed out luggage will have 4 large, empty suitcases to deal with. And you won't want to be tripping over those suitcases each time you get up to walk around your RV. There are a couple of possibilities for avoiding that problem, but you'll need to know which you are going to select in advance. To wait until after you arrive at your pick up point is too late. (Are you starting to see a pattern here?)

Dealer Storage of Empty Luggage. One option is to ask your dealer, in advance, if they can make available space for the storage of empty luggage. (Some will, some won't.) This is in many ways the simplest of solutions. You take possession of your rental unit, unpack, and leave your luggage at the dealers. You allow a little extra time for packing on your return and that's pretty much all there is to it.

Folding Duffels. Another option which overall is can work out equally well is to pack in duffle bags which you can collapse, fold or rollup after they are empty. There are a couple of disadvantages to this option. The first being that few will have four large, empty duffel bags sitting around, so this option involves making some extra purchases. A second disadvantage is that duffels of the type which will roll up really small are also generally lacking wheels. Schlepping 200 pounds of luggage plus a couple of carryons, without wheels, around an airport can be a big nuisance.

Shipping Considerations. A final option exists for winding up with you and an appropriate amount of stuff all in the right place and at the right time.

You can box up everything that is a problem to bring on the airplane and ship it one direction or the other or both.

Can You Ship Boxes to Dealer? One simple possibility, if it is OK with your dealer, is to put together a box or two or three of stuff and ship it to your dealer where you can pick it up when you arrive. This of course involves obtaining the approval of your dealer and requires that you plan far enough in advance to assure that your shipment will get to where it needs to be before you do.

There are a number of variations on this theme. You can assemble or buy stuff where you now live, ship it to your dealer, and at the end of your trip you can box it up and ship it back to yourself. Depending on the value of the stuff in question, and the trouble involved in return shipping, at the end of your trip you might also simply decide to throw away the extra stuff or to donate it to a local charitable organization.

Another variation on the buy and ship theme: We find a number of RV rental vacationers who choose to wait until they are living in their rental RV to figure out exactly what they need. They then buy items locally on an "as needed" basis and box them up and ship them home at the end of their trip.

$AVING$ TIP$

The Fly/Drive RV Vacationer Needs to Give Extra Thought to Souvenir Sorts of Purchases. Not only is there an up-front cost to such purchases, but there are often extra expenses involved in getting items home. You can spend your way into a position where the only option is to box up items and ship them home – an option which costs both extra dollars and valuable vacation time.

In our earlier discussions about the place of stuff in the plans of the RVer who is renting locally, we suggested that a rule of thumb might be "if in doubt, throw it in". In the case of the fly/drive traveler, trying to coordinate the presence of too much stuff can overly, and unnecessarily, complicate your journey. The point of stuff is to make your journey more pleasant, not less. For the fly/drive traveler, our suggested rule of thumb is, "if in doubt, leave it out". As we mentioned earlier in this section, if you error in leaving out something you later discover to be of importance, the odds are you will be able to buy whatever it is wherever you are.

Opening to the possibilities of a fly/drive vacation increases your options dramatically. The added difficulties of a fly/drive RV vacation are, in the overall picture, really pretty minor. If your dream destination is one requiring a fly/drive approach to the RV rental process, don't be put off by the added complications.

Chapter Fifteen
Special Considerations
Traveling With Pets

RVing WITH THE WHOLE FAMILY

*P*arrots look out of RV windows, guinea pigs on picnic tables for a breath of fresh air, cats check out campgrounds on their leashes. Ferrets, hamsters and gerbils, snakes and turtles, even fish – all are traveling the country in RVs as you are reading this. Precisely how much these travelers are enjoying their nomadic lifestyles is perhaps an open subject, but the fact that their human family members enjoy having them along is beyond question.

For purposes of our brief discussion here, and with apologies to our other-than-canine friends, we are going to assume "RVing with pet" means bringing along the family dog. More than 40% of dog owning RVers take the family pet along when they head out in their RVs. The idea of going on vacation, or even on a weekend getaway, without these special family members is simply unacceptable. For the RV renter, the situation is a bit more complex; however, in many cases Fido can be included on your rental RV vacation.

Dogs as traveling companions. The most obvious and most common of animal RVing companions is the family dog. Given the general fondness dogs have for "going for a ride" it is easy to understand their joy at being included in the family vacation – a ride lasting a week or two or more. Dogs are, generally speaking, both the most appreciative and the easiest of RV traveling companions.

Rental unit considerations. If your intention is to travel with your pet, you have a couple of issues to explore before making your final commitment to a rental unit. Specifically, does the dealer you have selected to this point allow traveling with pets and what extra costs and/or deposits are required?

Many RV rental dealers allow pets in their units. Many, but not all. It is essential that you ask up front. Don't just show up with your pet assuming it will all work out. Make certain your advance rental agreement specifies that you are bringing a pet.

Be specific when asking. Explain exactly what sort of pet (usually dog or cat) you are wanting to travel with . . . and how many. If your pet is a dog, be specific as to the size of your dog when talking to the dealer representative. Be up front with the representative. Don't obtain an OK for one small dog and then show up with three dogs – each the size of a cow – assuming no one will notice the difference.

Expect there to be extra costs involved. Some dealers will charge a flat fee, some will charge an extra cleaning and/or damage deposit, some will charge both. If you are required to pay some form of extra deposit, be clear up front as to exactly what must happen for you to get your deposit back.

$AVING$ TIP$

Some Campgrounds Charge Extra for Pets. Seldom are the charges major, but they can add up over the course of a one or two week vacation. Place a quick call and ask about extra charges for pets before committing to a specific campground.

Rules of the Road . . . With Pets

Traveling with a pet requires understanding some specific guidelines and a willingness to accept a few inconveniences. Here are some things to expect:

Campground Considerations

Living in a campground with your pet and close to others – some with pets and some without – requires special consideration.

First know that you will find in your travels a variety of responses. Varying degrees of acceptance await the traveling pet. Some campgrounds will not allow pets under any circumstances; some will have special areas set aside for those traveling with pets and many will charge extra fees. You will deal with special pet walking areas and a universal expectation that you pick up after your pet.

Leash requirements. Those campgrounds that do allows pets will almost always have a requirement that your pet be on a leash and under your control at all times. You will find this to be true in private/commercial campgrounds and in public campgrounds. Don't assume you will be allowed to let your pet to run free – no matter how much you and your pet would enjoy it.

Persistence in exercising your pet off leash will produce hostile stares, perhaps an administrative warning from those operating the camping area, and could lead to your being asked to leave the campground permanently. Don't say we didn't warn you.

If a requirement that your pet be on leash at all times would "ruin" the vacation for both of you, you should rethink the idea of bringing your pet along.

Inquire in ADVANCE. Because of the variation in pet rules from one campground to another, always find out the policies of your intended stopping place in advance. It is seldom a good idea to simply assume your know. In the Florida State Park System as an example, there are some campgrounds which allow pets and others which don't. Make it a habit to ask in advance.

Use Common Sense. There is pretty much nothing you could do, other than perhaps dumping raw sewage on the ground, which would annoy your camping neighbors more than going off for a day's sightseeing and leaving a barking dog behind to entertain the neighbors. Dealing with your pet in a campground is mostly a matter of common sense. Unfortunately pet owners singularly lacking in common sense may have preceded you and left behind an atmosphere of pet intolerance.

The issue of what to do with Fido while sightseeing is perhaps the most difficult one in the entire RVing with pet arena. You should **never** leave your friend in a closed car or RV on a hot, sunny day. You should never leave a pet prone towards barking unattended, even in an air conditioned RV with the windows shut, in a campground. And there are many attractions which are not pet tolerant. In some areas you may be able to find a kennel where you can leave your dog while you are out sightseeing. Again, don't count on it unless you have made advance inquiries.

Other Considerations

If your pet requires specific food, and particularly if your pet requires a specific food which is not universally available, be sure to bring along enough to last the duration of your trip. If your pet requires medications, add them to your checklist so they are not forgotten in the last minute rush to get on the road.

A good rule to thumb when it comes to water is to simply not expect your pet to drink water which you wouldn't drink. If you are drinking bottled water, provide bottled water for your pet. We accept there might be worse things than being closed up in a small RV with a pet who has diarrhea, though no examples come to mind at the moment.

Simply put, bringing the family pet along on vacation will restrict your enjoyment of other aspects of the trip. Having the pet along may or may not be worth it. It's a call only you can make.

Chapter Sixteen
Other Special Circumstances

*T*here are potential RVers who have excluded the rental RV possibility because of special needs or preferences. Our points in this short chapter are the suggestion that RV vacations are often available to those with special requirements and the recommendation that no one discount the possibility without first doing some investigating.

ADA Friendly Rental Vehicles Are Available.

Simply put, a special physical need of yours or of a member of your party does not necessarily exclude an RV adventure.

Cruise America, as an example, offers specially designed, wheelchair accessible units at some of their locations. These "FunMovers" feature power life gates, wider doors to the rear living space and bathroom, and assist handles in the bathroom. Contact Cruise America for details on these ADA friendly units.

Cruise America has clearly taken steps to expand accessibility of the RV lifestyle. Other RV rental outlets have made similar moves. Our point here is to suggest that you not allow special needs to eliminate the RV lifestyle from consideration. Do some investigating.

Future RVers With Allergies

The potential RVer with pet or smoke allergies or sensitivities should also make time to do a bit of investigating.

As discussed in the previous chapter, many rental RV dealers allow pets to join their owners on vacation. It follows that the future RV renter with pet allergies or special sensitivities should be specific about their requirements when talking with dealer representatives.

Don't Give Up on the RV Dream

Repeating, our point here is to encourage those interested in the RV life style, and who have discarded the possibility because of special needs or preferences, to give the possibility some additional study. Make a few phone calls. Send off a few e-mails. You won't know unless you ask. It is possible the wonderful world of RV travel is just around the corner for you.

Epilogue

The RV industry in general, and the RV rental industry in particular, are continually changing as they adjust to shifts in consumer preferences. Given this constant state of fluctuation, it is also true that <u>this book will be in constant and never ending revision</u>. You will find revisions, updates and corrections posted on a regular basis on our web site at <u>www.RVRentalGuide.com</u>.

We thank those readers who have provided constructive feedback. Know that your comments will serve to create future editions of this book which are intended to be continually improving in their ability to introduce others to the joys of traveling by rental RV.

Finally, we acknowledge there are some of you who will be seeking more in depth information about living in a rental RV. For you we are preparing other works which some will find helpful:

1. TRAVEL PLANNING FOR THE RV RENTER – Included in the book you are now holding, "RV Rentals", are the checklists and forms most commonly requested by those preparing for, and traveling on, a vacation in a rental RV. We recognize there are many who would like to take their organizational efforts to a higher level. For those travelers we have developed a workbook titled **"TRAVEL PLANNING FOR THE RV RENTER"**. This is *THE WORKBOOK you need* to lead you step-by-step through the planning process.

Inside you will find forms to assist in planning every aspect of your trip: Pre-planning, Activity Planning, Menu Planning and <u>more than 30 Checklists</u>. We have included an RV Adventure Journal, an Address Book, and even a few forms to help you use what you learn on your RV vacation to start planning your next RV outing.

2. RV KITCHENS – If you plan to do some cooking during your RV vacation, you should consider this book. *You have not selected an ordinary sort of vacation – don't settle for ordinary food.* Here you will find more than 100 recipes . . . each specifically developed for RV Kitchens (or anyone with a small kitchen, limited pantry space and a greater interest in being outside watching the sunset than inside hanging out in the kitchen)!

Loaded with suggestions for equipping, and effectively using, each of the RVer's four primary food preparation areas – the campfire, the grill, the picnic table and, of course, the RV's inside kitchen. The emphasis in this book is on preparing unique and interesting one dish meals which require total cooking time of 30 minutes or less.

To order either of these publications, or for more detailed information about pricing and availability, please go to <u>www.RVRentalGuide.com</u>.

In closing, let us be the first to welcome you to the RV life style. We again salute you for the sense of adventure and curiosity which has delivered you to this point. As we think back over our years of self contained travel, we realize we wouldn't trade them for anything . . . except perhaps to once again be standing where you are: at the very beginning of the journey.

Remember, **The Journey IS the Destination!** See you on the road!

Best wishes,

Dave & Kay

Appendixes

Appendix A

Forms & Worksheets

Initial "Possibles" List

Dealer: _____

Contact: _____

Address: _____

City: _____ **State:** _____ **Zip:** _____

Phone: _____ **eMail:** _____

Fax: _____ **Web Site:** _____

Dealer: _____

Contact: _____

Address: _____

City: _____ **State:** _____ **Zip:** _____

Phone: _____ **eMail:** _____

Fax: _____ **Web Site:** _____

Dealer: _____

Contact: _____

Address: _____

City: _____ **State:** _____ **Zip:** _____

Phone: _____ **eMail:** _____

Fax: _____ **Web Site:** _____

Dealer: _____

Contact: _____

Address: _____

City: _____ **State:** _____ **Zip:** _____

Phone: _____ **eMail:** _____

Fax: _____ **Web Site:** _____

Dealer: _____

Contact: _____

Address: _____

City: _____ **State:** _____ **Zip:** _____

Phone: _____ **eMail:** _____

Fax: _____ **Web Site:** _____

Dealer Questionnaire

(Make one copy for each dealer on your "possibles list")

Dealer Name:
Phone Number:
Web Site:
eMail:

1. **I am a first-time RV renter. I am thinking about renting a** (type of unit) **and am looking for something around** (size) **feet long. Which units in your inventory come closest to meeting my criteria?**

2. **I am planning to vacation for** (length of time) **around** (date). **How is you availability in that time frame?**

3. **If I can be flexible in my time frame and/or the type of unit I am looking for, what sorts of money saving specials are available?**

4. **What are your insurance requirements? Insurance recommendations?**

5. **Does the base price of your units include everything I'll need to go RVing?**

6. **What sort of total costs are we looking at?**

7. **Is there anything else I should, could, or have to pay to your firm . . . anything at all?**

8. **Why would I be better off dealing with your firm than one of your competitors?**

DEALER COMPARISON WORKSHEET

Dealer Name	Inventory	Availability	Personality	Inclusions	Total Costs	Ranking

Remarks:

QUESTIONS SOME DEALERS PREFER YOU DON'T ASK

1. How soon can you provide copies of all paperwork, <u>everything I will be required to sign</u>, for my attorney's review?

2. What would be my daily mileage allowance and what am I charged per mile for exceeding that?

3. What, other than my base rental fee and mileage charges, could I be asked to pay to your company?

4. Are there any state or local taxes or fees which haven't been included in my total?

5. What sort of roadside assistance, for mechanical problems, is provided?

6. If my unit breaks down during my vacation, will I be provided a replacement at no additional cost to me?

7. Specifically what insurance coverage is included in my base rental fee? What other insurance coverages are required? What other insurance coverages are recommended?

8. Does my base rental fee include everything I will need to live in my RV? How much extra will it cost me for a unit I can actually live in?

9. How old is the average unit in your fleet? What is the average total mileage on your units?

10. Do you allow smoking in your units? Can you provide a smoke-free unit?

11. What sorts of deposits will I be required to pay? Exactly what must happen for my deposits to be refunded?

12. Do you have an area where we can clean our unit before we turn it in? Do you have a dumping station available for the use of your rental customers?

13. Do you allow pets in your units? Can you provide a unit which has been pet free?

14. How many miles per gallon can I expect?

RV RENTAL
Trip Planning Workbook

Dates of Travel

Primary Destination

Signature Event   **Date(s)**

Rental Dealer Information

Dealer	
Contact Information	
Name	Phone
eMail	Fax
Emergency Number/Roadside Assistance	

Non-RV Transportation

Airline	Phone	Confirmation #	Destination	LV	AR

Car Rental	Phone	Confirmation #

Other	Phone	Confirmation #

Campground Information

AR	LV	Campground Name	Phone	Confirmation #	Ck In	Ck Out

DAY/DATE

Today's Travel Plans -

Travel From:	To:
Estimated Mileage:	Estimated Travel Time:
Route:	

Today's Activity Plans -

Our Campground Reservations -

Campground:	Phone:
Directions:	

Today's Meal Plans -

Breakfast:

Lunch:

Dinner:

DAY/DATE

Today's Travel Plans -

Travel From:	To:
Estimated Mileage:	Estimated Travel Time:
Route:	

Today's Activity Plans -

Our Campground Reservations -

Campground:	Phone:
Directions:	

Today's Meal Plans -

Breakfast:

Lunch:

Dinner:

Campground Scouting Report

Name:

Date: | **Location:**

Directions:

Amenities:

Favorite Sites:

Number	PT/BI*	Remarks	Views	Shade	E	W	S

Comments:

* Pull Through or Back In Site

Appendix B

Checklists

Checklists

A couple of opening points about checklists:

1. Love them or hate them, there is no way of getting around it – you are going to be using checklists as you prepare for and journey on your RV rental vacation. The question is not one of using or not using checklists. The questions are will you be using lists of your own design or someone else's and will they be ones you attempt to retain mentally or will they be written?

2. In our experience, no checklist is ever perfect. No group of checklists is all inclusive. We have spent decades developing and refining the lists we use and still find we are making adjustments, additions and deletions. At this point in your RV experience, we suggest you are best served by looking for checklists which seem to be good starting points. Don't waste your time trying to find, or develop, lists which are perfect. Such perfection doesn't exist . . . and even if it did it is unlikely you would recognize it without having first experienced the RV lifestyle.

As mentioned, checklists can be either written or mental. A mental list requires a sharply focused mind – a rare thing in our household during the hectic time preceding a new RV adventure. We strongly recommend the use of written checklists – ours, ours as modified by you, or lists of your own design. The important thing is not the source of your lists. The important thing is to use the lists you have – every time, NO EXCEPTIONS.

$AVING$ TIP$

Use Checklists. Forgetting important stuff can be both inconvenient and expensive.

Basic Equipment Checklist

Any notion of a *complete* basic equipment list for an RV is a classic oxymoron. The implication being there is some sort of brief, but adequate, way of equipping an RV. We have to the conclusion that RVs are never fully equipped. We need only to casually thumb through a Camping World catalog to identify several new, previously unknown, and now essential accessories.

Clearly the idea of a "complete, basic" list is one that doesn't make sense. The lists on the following page detail those items we would think essential were we given an empty RV and a minimal allowance for equipping it.

Some of these essentials should be – or at least are likely to be – provided by your dealer. Those items are on the list in italics. Think of this checklist as a starting point. Delete those items which make no sense to you and add those which would make your RV vacation both special and more personal.

Basic Equipment List
For the RV Renter

Essential	Nice to Have
☐ Address Book	☐ Axe
☐ Campground Guide	☐ Beach Towels
☐ *Chemicals for Black Water Tank*	☐ Binoculars
☐ Disposable Rubber Gloves	☐ Books & Magazines
☐ *Electrical Adapters*	☐ Broom & Dust Pan
☐ *Fire Extinguisher*	☐ Calling Card
☐ First Aid Kit *	☐ Camera
☐ Flashlight & Spare Batteries	☐ Cell Phone & Power Cord
☐ Insect Repellent	☐ Duct Tape
☐ Level	☐ Folding Shovel
☐ Leveling Blocks or Boards	☐ Lawn Chairs
☐ Maps	☐ Lantern
☐ *Sewer Hose with Fittings*	☐ Laundry Bag
☐ Sunscreen or Sun Block	☐ Pens, Pencils & Paper
☐ Tire Gauge	☐ Playing Cards, Games
☐ *Water Hose, Fresh Water (White)*	☐ Travel Clock
☐ *Water Pressure Regulator*	☐ Travel Journal
☐ Wheel Chocks	☐ "Walkman" Type CD Player
☐	☐ CD's
☐	☐ Water Filter

* Band-Aids, Antiseptic Ointment, Gauze, Aspirin, Tweezers, Sunburn Relief Spray, etc.

Dealer Delivery Checklist

D-Day (Delivery Day). There is no point in the RV rental process where so many things requiring your attention, or at least your acknowledgement, come from so many different directions in such a short amount of time. And there are probably few points in the entire process where you are more distracted, less able to focus. If this Delivery Day stuff were simple, boring, everyday kind of stuff, you could simply pay no attention and figure out whatever you missed later. The problem is that much of this is important information – information which can significantly impact your entire vacation.

So how do you keep on track? How can you be certain you catch at least the most fundamental parts of what you need to know? You guessed it – lists are the answer!

As a starting point, you will be certain to have questions. If you fail to write them down, it is at least equally certain that you will forget to ask at least a few of them. The following three page checklist will serve to remind you of some of the important things you will want to cover during the orientation and delivery process. Many of these things will be happening at the same time – and to the general state of confusion you can add a knowing that the events which take place won't do so in the order they are listed.

$AVING$ TIP$

Importance of Delivery Checklist. A delivery checklist, ours or one of your own, can help to jog your memory during the confusion and excitement surrounding the process of taking delivery of your home on wheels and getting started on your vacation. Thoroughly check the physical condition of your unit and confirm the presence of all agreed upon inclusions.

There will be three differing sorts of activities taking place at more or less the same time:

Dealer Orientation: A representative of your dealer will take you through your new home and will give you an item-by-item orientation and explanation of how things work. Things that will – or at least should – be covered during this orientation are indicated on the following lists with the letter "**O**".

Survey/Inspection: As you are going through the RV, you will want to be watching for things which are damaged and/or not working properly. Any such items/areas should be noted on your paperwork before you sign anything. Areas worthy of special attention are indicated with the letter **"S"**.

Inclusions Inventory: Finally, at the same time you are getting oriented and looking for flaws, you will also want to be sure that everything which is supposed to be included is on board. Items to watch for are identified with an **"I"** on your checklists.

Everything listed on the following four pages is important. That it takes four pages to cover it all is perhaps the best argument of all favoring the use of checklists!

Dealer Delivery Checklist

	OUTSIDE (O = Orientation, S = Survey, I = Inventory)	
✓	**Item**	**Notes**
	(S) Exterior cosmetic inspection. Particular attention to roof, wheel covers, front & rear bumpers.	
	(O/S/I) Storage compartment doors. Operational? Locks working? Keys included?	
	(O/I) How does entry step work? Entry door? Screen door? Do locks work? Keys included?	
	(O) How the hydraulic leveling jacks work (if applicable)?	
	(O) How to operate hood & check fluid levels? Where is fuel fill?	
	(O) Where is the chassis/vehicle battery? The coach/house battery? Battery disconnects?	
	(O) Operation and location of outside lights and electrical outlets.	
	(O/I) Location of LP Gas (Propane) Tank(s)? Are they full? How are they refilled?	
	(O/I) Where is the spare tire? The jack? Warning triangles, flares?	
	(O) Where are the furnace vent, the refrigerator access panel, cable TV hookup (if applicable) and the stove vent cover? How does the stove vent cover operate?	
	(O/I) Where is the city water inlet? How do you connect to city water? Be sure you have a fresh water hose and a water pressure regulator (if required or recommended by your dealer).	
	(O) Is there an outside shower? How does it operate?	

✓	Item	Notes
	(O/S) Where is the fresh water tank, the water pump? How does the water pump operate? How do you fill the fresh water tank? Is there enough water in the tank?	
	(O) Where is the water heater? How does it operate electrically, with propane?	
	(O/S/I) Where are the valves for dumping (emptying) the holding tanks? What is the procedure for dumping? Check to be sure tanks are empty. Where is the sewer hose?	
	(O/I) Where is the 120-volt electrical cord? How do you connect to "shore power"? Where are the electrical adapters?	
	(O) Review location and operation of Generator (if applicable).	
	(O/S) Cosmetic inspection of awning (if applicable). How does it work?	

DRIVER'S COMPARTMENT
(O = Orientation, S = Survey, I = Inventory)

✓	Item	Notes
	(O) Review the operation of any unfamiliar controls or instruments.	
	(O) How do you adjust mirrors and seats?	
	(O) If your unit is equipped with a backup/rear vision camera, be sure you understand how it works.	

INSIDE
(O = Orientation, S = Survey, I = Inventory)

✓	Item	Notes
	(O) If your unit is equipped with slide-outs, how do they operate?	

(O/I) Inside cosmetic inspection. Be sure to operate all faucets, windows and drawers. Review operation of emergency exit window(s).	
(O) Location and operation of monitor panel.	
(OI) Location of power distribution panel, circuit breakers and blade fuses. Are spare fuses included? Is so, where are they?	
(O) Location and operation of generator start switch and hour meter.	
(O) Review operation of 12-volt water pump. If your unit has a water filter, how does it work?	
(O) Location and operation of GFI outlets, interior lights, light switches and electrical outlets.	
(O) Wall switch(s) for water heater (both gas & electric if applicable).	
(O) Location and operation of carbon monoxide detector, smoke alarm, LP gas detector and fire extinguisher.	
(O) How do you operate the range/stove burners? The oven? Vent fan? Range Cover? The microwave and/or convection oven?	
(O) How does the refrigerator work? Is it on?	
(O) How do the furnace and air conditioner operate?	
(O) Where are exhaust fans and overhead vents located? How to they work?	
(I) Is a First Aid Kit included? If so, where is it?	
(O/I) Review operation of toilet and care of holding tank. Are holding tank chemicals included? What sort of toilet paper is recommended? Is it included?	
(O) How does the shower work?	
(O) How do you access storage areas under the bed or beneath the sofa or the bench seats in the dinette?	

(O) How do the convertible sleeping areas work? (sofa, dinette or other areas which serve multiple functions).	
(O) Review the operation of any entertainment systems included in your unit. TV, antenna, cable hookup, satellite system, stereo, VCR or DVD player.	
(I) Inventory **Personal Kits** if provided by dealer.	
(I) Inventory **Vehicle/Kitchen Kit** if provided by dealer.	
(I) Double check that all items on the dealer's list of inclusions are somewhere in the RV.	
REVIEW & SIGN ALL PAPERWORK	

Finally, because no matter how hard you try you won't be able to remember everything, be sure you know who to call when you find yourself in that inevitable mental cul-de-sac:

DEALER NAME _____

CONTACT NAME _____

DEALER PHONE NUMBER _____

EMERGENCY ROAD SERVICE PROVIDER _____

ERS PHONE NUMBER _____

Basic Kitchen Inventory
&
Preliminary Shopping List – Consumables

The following two lists cover a highly personal area of equipping the rental RV. The opening question is one of how you want your RV kitchen set up – which is of course dependant on how and how much you plan to use it. The second list addresses the related, but generally separate, question of what sort of consumables you want to have in your home on wheels. Given that there are not answers to either question which are equally true for all RVers, it follows that there are no checklists which are universally valid for all styles of RV living.

The **"Basic Kitchen Inventory"** checklist is extracted from our way of doing things. It is a highly condensed version of what is in our RV's kitchen right now. Of necessity it is a reflection of the way we like to do things. This list will serve as the basis for the assembling of a list of your own. The single best bit of advice we can give you is this: Pay attention to what it is you really use in your "sticks and bricks" kitchen. Those things you use on a regular basis are the sorts of things you will want with you in your rental RV.

The **"Preliminary Shopping List – Consumables"** is also a thing to be personalized. Most of you will want most of the things on the list we have provided. Few, if any, of you will find everything we have suggested appropriate.

$AVING$ TIP$

Don't Buy Snacks At Convenience Stores. Plan to keep adequate supplies of snacks and drinks in your RV. When inventories start to run low, replenish the pantry at a super market – not in a convenience store.

On the Consumables list, we include the **"Spice Bag"**. Those of you who have not yet read **Chapter 8 – The Rental RV Kitchen** (and those who have read it, but didn't find it particularly memorable) are wondering what the heck a "Spice Bag" is. In Chapter 8, we suggested that the one area of pantry stocking where it is wise to be over-supplied is in the selection of spices. Since you already have the spices you most frequently use in your cupboard at home, the thought is that you bring some of them along. Throw a dozen or so of your favorites – you know which ones they are – in a resealable plastic bag. Spices are a cost effective and space efficient way to add variety to your RV meals.

Finally, we acknowledge those of you who intend to eat out most, or all, of the time. While you might want to glance at the following two lists, you can easily ignore 80% to 90% of what their recommendations.

Basic Kitchen Inventory
for the RV Renter

Essential

- ☐ 3 Quart Covered Sauce Pan
- ☐ 12" Covered Skillet (Nonstick)
- ☐ Can Opener
- ☐ Coffee Pot
- ☐ Corkscrew
- ☐ Knife, Small Paring
- ☐ Knife, Large Carving
- ☐ Measuring Cup
- ☐ Measuring Spoons
- ☐ "Shaker Jar"
- ☐ Spatula
- ☐ Spoon, Mixing/Serving
- ☐ Spoon, Slotted
- ☐ Vegetable Peeler
- ☐ Small Whisk
- ☐ Zester/Grater
- ☐
- ☐
- ☐
- ☐
- ☐

Nice to Have

- ☐ BBQ Tongs
- ☐ Bottle Opener
- ☐ Campfire Roasting Forks
- ☐ Charcoal – Match Light
- ☐ Charcoal Grill – Small
- ☐ Coffee Bean Grinder
- ☐ Electric Skillet
- ☐ Mixing Bowls
- ☐ Propane Stove
- ☐ Slow Cooker/Crock Pot
- ☐
- ☐
- ☐
- ☐
- ☐
- ☐
- ☐
- ☐
- ☐
- ☐

Preliminary Shopping List
Consumables

Supplies

- ☐ Paper/Plastic Plates/Bowls
- ☐ Plastic Glasses/Cups
- ☐ Plastic Utensils
- ☐ Heavy Duty Aluminum Foil
- ☐ Coffee Filters
- ☐ Dish Detergent
- ☐ Matches
- ☐ Napkins
- ☐ Paper Towels
- ☐ Plastic Wrap
- ☐ Resealable Food Storage Bags
- ☐ Tablecloth
- ☐ Toilet Paper
- ☐ Trash Bags
- ☐ All Purpose Cleaner
- ☐
- ☐
- ☐
- ☐
- ☐
- ☐

Pantry Basics*

- ☐ BBQ Sauce/Steak Sauce
- ☐ Bread
- ☐ Butter/Margarine
- ☐ Canned or Frozen Vegetables
- ☐ Canned Beef Stew/Chili/Soup
- ☐ Canned Chicken/Tuna/Salmon
- ☐ Coffee/Tea/Hot Cocoa Mix
- ☐ Cold Cereal/Oatmeal
- ☐ Eggs
- ☐ Energy Bars
- ☐ Equal/Splenda/Sugar
- ☐ Ketchup/Mayo/Mustard/Pickles
- ☐ Milk
- ☐ Peanut Butter
- ☐ Salad Dressing
- ☐ Salsa
- ☐ Salt & Pepper
- ☐ Snacks
- ☐ Soft Drinks/Powdered Drink Mix
- ☐ Microwave Popcorn
- ☐ Spice Bag (From Home)

* NOTE: Make certain to pick up at least enough food for two meals – your first evening and first breakfast.

Campground Departure
Inside & Outside Lists

There is often a lot of drama in campground departures. Much purposeful and determined pacing around accompanied by head scratching and serious, contemplative stares at items on which the RVer knows action should be taken – but is unable to remember precisely what that action might be.

Here's the thing about campground departures: Without the use of a checklist there is more opportunity for serious error (meaning mistakes leading to significant property damage or personal injury) than in perhaps any other part of the RVing experience:

If you forget to buy or pack an item of importance, you can either do without or pickup whatever it is your next stop at the store.

If you fail to hookup something when you arrive at your campsite, the omission will make itself know the first time you try to use whatever is dependent on the thing you didn't hookup.

If there is an aspect of the dealer orientation which you failed to absorb, you have the options of looking it up in your manual or asking a neighboring RVer.

In other words, most things you forget to do during your RVing experience cause some inconvenience, but are generally without serious consequences.

Some steps, if forgotten in your departure sequence, have the potential to cause major problems.

Our advice – and our personal practice:

ALWAYS USE DEPARTURE CHECKLISTS
EVERYTIME, NO EXCEPTIONS!!

Campground Departure
Inside List

KITCHEN AREA	✓	✓	✓	✓	✓	✓	✓	✓	✓	✓	✓	✓	✓	✓
Cabinets & Drawers – CLOSED														
Counters – STOW/SECURE ALL ITEMS														
Microwave Turntable - SECURED														
Pantry – CONTENTS SECURED														
Pantry Door - LATCHED														
Pilot Lights – OFF														
Refrigerator – CONTENTS SECURED														
Refrigerator Door - LATCHED														
Small Appliances – STOWED/SECURED														
Range Top Cover – CLOSED														
LIVING/DINING AREA														
Antenna - RETRACT														
Dining Table – CLEAR														
Furnace/Air Conditioner Thermostat - OFF														
BEDROOM/BATH														
Doors & Drawers – CLOSED														
Nightstand – CLEARED														
Shower Door - SECURED														
Water Pump – OFF														
MISCELLANEOUS														
Ceiling Vents														
Television(s) – SECURED														
Water Heater - OFF														

Windows, Blinds - SECURED														
Windows – SHUT														
Take Out Trash														
Final Walk Through														
Slideouts – RETRACTED														

Campground Departure
Outside List

	✓	✓	✓	✓	✓	✓	✓	✓	✓	✓	✓	✓	✓	✓
Awning – RETRACTED & LOCKED														
TV Cable – REMOVE & STOW														
"Basement" Doors – SECURED/LOCKED														
Dump Valves/Cap - CLOSED & SECURED														
Electric Cable/Accessories – STOWED														
LP GAS Valves – OFF*														
Sewer Hose/Accessories – STOWED														
Stove Vent – SECURE LOCKING TABS														
Water Heater – OFF														
Fresh Water Tank – FILL ¼ FULL														
Water Hose/Regulator - STOW														
Outside Water Connections - COVER														
BBQ Grill/Stove/Propane Bottle - STOW														
Doormat/Rug – PUT AWAY														
Lawn Furniture – PUT AWAY														
Outside Plaques/Lights - STOW														
Levelers/Jacks/Blocks/Chocks - STOW														
Stabilizer Jacks – UP														
Tire Pressure & Lug Nuts - CHECK														
Mirrors & Driver's Seat – ADJUST														
Door – LOCKED														

Slidouts – RETRACTED														
Steps – RETRACTED														
VERIFY MANEUVERING CLEARANCE														

PULL FORWARD, STOP, GET OUT, CHECK CAMPSITE

Did You Forget Anything?														
Is The Site Clean?														

* Turning off the LP Gas is a safety issue. If you plan to run your refrigerator on LP Gas while traveling, know that it won't cool if you turn off the gas.

Dealer Return Checklist

Compared to the time you took delivery – with all the paperwork and stuff to go over and things to figure out – the process of returning your RV rental to the dealer is really pretty simple. Basically the dealer expects the unit to be returned in clean, re-rentable condition – and with all of their stuff in it and none of yours. In simple terms, everything which was full when you took delivery should be full when you return the vehicle. Everything which was empty should be empty. Everything which was clean should be clean. At the time you accepted delivery you learned what needs to happen for you to get back your deposit(s). That pretty much provides your map for getting the unit ready to return. Here are some items to help jog your memory:

✔	Item
	RETURN UNIT ON TIME
	Holding Tanks should be empty
	Gas Tank should be full
	Water Tank should be empty
	Propane Tank(s) should be full
	Unit should be clean – Specifically:
	All dishes, utensils, pots and pans should be washed and dried
	Wipe down all floors and countertops
	Wipe out inside of cabinets and drawers
	Empty pantry and refrigerator
	Range, oven and microwave should be clean
	Clean kitchen sink
	Clean toilet and bathroom sink
	Clean inside of all windows
	Remove all personal property – double check to be sure nothing is left behind.
	NOTE: Most dealers <u>do not</u> require that linens in their personal and vehicle kits be freshly laundered at the time they are returned. Confirm with your dealer at the time of delivery.

Concluding Thoughts ~ Checklists

In this Appendix we have included the seven checklists most requested by RV rental vacationers. The list are not all inclusive, but should be adequate at this stage in your RV rental experience. Few of these lists are strictly necessary; all have the potential to enhance a specific aspect of your rental RV vacation.

For those seeking a higher level of organization, we recommend our workbook **"Trip Planning for the RV Renter"**. In that publication we have included the seven checklists found here . . . plus another two dozen. A total of 31 checklists to help organize virtually every aspect of your RV experience! The workbook also contains forms to help you Pre-Plan your trip, Plan Activities, and worksheets for designing Menu Plans and their related Grocery Shopping Lists. You will even find an RV Adventure Journal, an Address Book, and a few forms to help you use what you learn on this RV vacation to start planning your next RV outing. Though perhaps not absolutely essential, many interested in really getting their vacationing "act together" – and keeping it together – have found this workbook to be the key to planning a successful RV rental vacation.

Appendix C

Glossary

Glossary

Black Water Holding Tank – This is the where the waste (sewage) goes when you flush the toilet. You will want to add chemicals to this tank to help control odors and to aid in the breakdown of solid materials. This tank should be emptied periodically at either a **Dump Station** or into a sewer hookup at your campsite. The **Black Water Tank** is most commonly located beneath the floor of the RV.

Boondocking, Dry Camping, Primitive Camping – Camping without water, electrical or sewer hookups. In place of these hookups, boondockers rely on "on-board" systems such as generators, batteries, a fresh water tank and holding tanks

Bunkhouse – Refers to an RV floor plan which has bunk beds – typically in addition to regular beds. **Bunkhouse** arrangements are especially popular with families with children.

Caravan - A group of RVers traveling together is called an RV **Caravan**. Commercial caravans offer wonderful supporting services and are a marvelous way to see a lot in a comparatively short period of time. Some RV rental dealers allow their units to go into Mexico if part of an approved commercial caravan.

Class A Motorhome – They are the largest of the self-propelled RVs and are often seen as resembling buses. Class As are built on specially designed chassis. The less extravagant of these units are generally available at RV rental dealers and are a popular choice with RV renters. Sizes run from around 20 feet to over 40 feet.

Class B Motorhome - Also called Camper Vans/Camping Van Conversions, these are the smallest of the drivable RVs. The starting point for these units is a conventional van . . . and a great plus to the Class B is that it drives pretty much like a conventional van. Some feature raised roofs, some custom bodies, but they remain the easiest of the RVs to drive. Many fit in regular parking spaces and they are comparatively easy on gas.

Class C Motorhome – Also known as "mini-motorhomes" or simply "mini", the most recognizable feature of the **Class C** is the distinctive cab-over bunk. Built on a cutaway van chassis, the **Class C** combines the conveniences of the Class A with the drivability of the Class B . . . and at a price lower than either. No wonder it's the most popular and widely available of rental RVs!

Cockpit - The driving area in a self-propelled RV. As might be expected, the **Cockpit** is where you will find the pilot (driver) and co-pilot (navigator).

Converter – Many items in an RV, such as interior lights, fans and the water pump, operate on 12-volt DC power at all times. **Converters** insure a continuous supply of 12-volt power by transforming/converting 120-volt AC power into 12-volt DC power when the RV is plugged into a 120-volt receptacle or connected to an AC generator.

Curbside - The "passenger side" of the RV. The side which faces the curb when parked. With very few exceptions, this is the side where the entrance door is located.

Dinette – Looking like a booth in a restaurant, the most common sort of dining area in the rental RV is the **Dinette**. Additional storage is usually found under the bench seats. Most dinettes can be converted into beds when additional sleeping space is needed.

Dinghy or Toad – A vehicle pulled behind a drivable RV. Occasionally the **Dinghy** will ride on a trailer or with two wheels on a special trailer called a "tow dolly". Most often the **Dinghy** is "flat-towed" with all four wheels on the ground.

Drivables – RVs which travel under their own motive power. Class A, B, and C motorhomes are all examples of drivables.

Dump Station – Found in most campgrounds, at some rest areas, and at other facilities offering services to RVers. It is simply a concrete pad with an opening into which the RVer empties – "Dumps" – the accumulated contents in their **Black Water Tank** and their **Gray Water Tank**. A **Sewer Hose** is used to connect the RV to this opening.

Fifth-Wheel Trailers - **Fifth Wheel Trailers** are designed to be towed by pickup and medium duty trucks equipped with a special hitch. These trailers have bi-level sort of design with the bedroom, or living room, in a raised area over the truck bed. Because they can only be towed by specially equipped vehicles, **Fifth Wheel Trailers** are seldom a reasonable option for the RV renter.

Fresh Water – Also called Potable Water. Water which is presumed to be safe for human consumption.

Fresh Water Tank – A large tank which enables the RVer to haul around a supply of **Fresh Water**. Some of these tanks are huge – up to 100 gallons and more. Unless you intend to be "**Boondocking**" for an extended period, it makes little sense to completely fill a large fresh water tank.

Full Hookup – A campsite offering electric, water and sewer connections. In some campgrounds, "**Full Hookup**" even includes cable TV and telephone.

Full-Timer – One who lives exclusively in their RV. Most **Full-Timers** do not have any sort of fixed/permanent "sticks and bricks" home. Estimates are that there are currently about 1,000,000 North Americans living full-time in RVs..

Galley – Much RV terminology finds its origin in our nautical counterparts. As an example, the **RV Kitchen** is frequently called the **Galley**.

Generator – Generators are usually fueled with gasoline or diesel fuel. A few are powered with propane, but such units are seldom found in rental RVs. Their purpose is to provide 120-volt AC power when it would not otherwise be available.

Gray Water Holding Tank – The kitchen sink, bathroom sinks and shower all drain into the **Gray Water Tank** or Tanks (some RVs have two **Gray Water Tanks**). Like the **Black Water Tank**, the **Gray Water Tank** will need to be emptied ("dumped") periodically. Like their black water counterparts, gray water tanks are typically located under the main floor of the RV.

Heat Strips – **Heat strips** are electric heating elements which can be located in an RV's air conditioning system. They use the air conditioner's fan and ducting system to distribute slightly warmed air. Using **heat strips** is a bit more effective than running around inside a cold RV waving a hair dryer, but not by much.

Hitch - The mechanical device which connects a unit being towed to the vehicle that pulls it.

Holding Tanks - Tanks that "hold" liquid wastes until the RV can be connected to a sewer. **Holding Tanks** include a **Gray Water Tank** to hold water from the sinks and shower and a **Black Water Tank** to hold sewage from the toilet.

Hookup - Connecting to a campground's utilities. See also "**Full Hookup**".

House Battery – Another name for the battery or batteries which provide 12-volt electrical power in the living area of a drivable RV. These batteries are separate from the vehicle battery used by the motive power portion of the motorhome.

Inverter – These devices transform 12-volt DC power into 120-volt AC power. While **inverter's** output ratings vary widely, even a small **inverter** can, if plugged into a cigarette lighter, provide enough "household" type power to operate a computer or a TV. Rarely would you find an **inverter** in a rental RV; however, if a consistent source of 120-volt power is important, an **inverter** might be the sort of thing you will want to bring along.

Kitchen Kit – Also called a **Vehicle Provisioning Kit.** These kits equip the RV kitchen in a minimal, but generally adequate sort of way. Particularly for the fly/drive RV renter, renting one of these kits from your dealer is much more convenient than trying to equip a kitchen with stuff you bring from home. Contents of these kits vary. If renting a **Kitchen Kit**, you should to get a list of items included from your dealer. See **"Personal Kit"**.

KOA – With more than 500 RV parks in North America, **Kampgrounds of America** offers both destination and overnight campground facilities for the vacationing RVer.

Leveling – The process of positioning an RV on campsite in such a way that it will be level is called **leveling**. Often leveling is a simple matter of parking the RV in just the right spot. In other situations leveling will require the use of ramps or wooden blocks placed under the wheels, of power leveling jacks, or of built-in scissors jacks.

Nonpotable Water – Water which is not safe for human consumption.

Park Model - These units are similar to large, conventional trailers, but are not designed for recreational travel. They are intended for permanent parking.

Part-Timers – **Part-timer** is the descriptive term applied to those who use their RVs more than for an annual, normal vacation, but less than full-time. See also: **"Full-Timer"**, **"Snowbird"**, and **"Weekender"**.

Personal Kit – These kits help to equip the rental RV for daily living. An option is to rent these kits from your rental RV dealer rather than bringing the stuff from home. Typically these kits include bedding, a pillow, a bath towel, dish towel and wash cloth. With some dealers the kit also includes an individual place setting of dishes and silverware. See **"Kitchen Kit"**.

Pilot Light – A small continuous flame in an oven, refrigerator, water heater, furnace or stove top. Its function is typically to light a propane appliance's main burner when heat is called for.

Pop-up, Tent Trailer, Fold-Down Camping Trailer, Folding Camping Trailer – all differing names for the same sort of recreational vehicle. These are lightweight units which collapse, or fold down, for storage and towing.

Propane – Also called LPG, LP Gas, liquefied petroleum gas, bottled gas and CPG (compressed petroleum gas). It is used in RVs for heating and cooking. It is also one of two, or three, power sources used for refrigeration.

Pull-through - A **Pull-Through** campsite is one which is open on both ends. The RVer pulls into the site driving forward and when the time comes to leave simply continues forward and exits the site on the other end – all without ever needing to back up.

Rig – Many RVers refer to their units as their "Rigs".

Roof Air Conditioning – This one is pretty simple! **Roof Air Conditioning** is an air conditioning unit mounted on the roof. **Roof Air Conditioning** is available to cool the RV anytime the RV is plugged into a campground's electrical system or when running a generator of adequate size.

RV – Stands for **Recreation Vehicle**, a general name applicable to all vehicles – both towables and drivables – containing living space. Several are RVs, the practice of using them is RVing, the people who use them are RVers.

Self-contained - An RV which contains all that is needed for normal short-term living without any need for external connections.

Sewer Hose – A large hose joining the RV to a campground's sewer connection or to the opening at an RV **Dump Station**. Used to empty **Holding Tanks** or to allow the direct flow of liquid wastes into the campground's sewage system.

Shore Cord – Another nautical term. This one simply refers to the cord used to plug the RV into a campground's electrical hookup.

Shore Power – Refers to the electricity provided to your RV when you have connected to an external source.

Slide-Out – **Slide-Outs** extend the RV's living space by using 12-volt DC electric motors, high pressure hydraulic systems, or some form of manual system to "slide-out" the walls of the RV in one or more places. **Slide-Outs** are only extended when the RV is stopped and setup for camping.

Snowbird – Anyone from a cold northern climate who heads south to warmer weather in the winter months. Over 1.1 million RVers are included in this group.

Streetside – The side of the vehicle which faces the street when parked.

Tailgunner – The last RV in a caravan is usually the **Tailgunner**. The **Tailgunner** follows the caravan and assists caravan members who have had mechanical problems or other road trouble.

Tail Swing – To the extent a motorhome has a long overhang extending behind its rear axle, it will be inclined to **"Tail Swing"** (a horizontal movement of the rear of the motorhome) when turned sharply. Tail swing happens either when the motorhome is moving forward or when it is in reverse. The rental RV driver will need to be conscious of the amount of tail swing occurring with their specific unit to avoid such disagreeable episodes as the striking of walls, parked vehicles and road signs.

Towable – An RV which is not self-propelled. **Towables** are *towed* from place to place.

Two-Way & Three-Way refrigerators (Also called Reefers) – RV refrigerators usually have several operating modes. A "two-way" refrigerator will operate on either propane or 120-volt AC (alternating current) – the same sort of electricity as in your "sticks and bricks" house. In addition to propane and AC power, a "three-way" refrigerator also is capable of operating on 12-volt DC (direct current) – the same as used in motor vehicles.

Tow Bar - Used to connect a dinghy/toad to a motorhome when it is to be "flat-towed". ie. When it is to be towed with all four wheels on the ground.

Toy-Hauler – A term applied to any sort of RV with built-in interior cargo space for motorcycles, ATVs, etc. Though **Toy-Haulers** appear most commonly in the form of conventional and fifth wheel trailers, a limited number are also being manufactured as Class A and Class C motorhomes.

Travel Trailer – Available in a huge range of sizes and configurations, the **Travel Trailer,** also known as the "Conventional Trailer", is perhaps the most popular of RVs. These trailers have an "A-Frame" with a coupler and are attached to a standard ball mount on the tow vehicle. Depending on the size of the trailer, and the tow rating of the vehicle, **Travel Trailers** can be pulled behind cars, mini-vans, SUVs or pickup trucks. Larger models require heavy duty tow vehicles.

Wagonmaster – A **Wagonmaster** is one who guides a caravan of RVs on a trip. Commercial caravans include a **Wagonmaster** who is hired to organize and lead the trip. On noncommercial caravans a **Wagonmaster** is often chosen or elected by the caravan members.

Wally World – A nickname for Wal-Mart, one of the most RV friendly companies in the country. If you hear an RVer say that they are going to **Wally World**, you know they're headed for Wal-Mart.

Weekenders - People who use their RVs primarily for weekends and vacations of more or less "normal" lengths.

Appendix D

Recommended Reading & Resources

Recommended Reading & Resources

Recommended Reading

Travel Planning for RV Renters
Dave & Kay Corby

Of course we recommend our own books! This one is the only planning guide available which is expressly designed for RV renters. Forms, worksheets, and checklists cover every aspect of the rental RV vacation – nothing is left to chance. More information is available at www.RVRentalGuide.com.

RV Kitchens
Dave & Kay Corby

More than just another cookbook! Here, in addition to over 100 recipes specifically developed for the RV Kitchen, you will find detailed information and suggestions for cooking in an RV kitchen. Find out what equipment you'll need to produce quality meals in 30 minutes or less. www.RVRentalGuide.com.

Trailer Life Directory

We list here the two most popular of the campground directories, **"Trailer Life"** *and* **"Woodall's"** *(listed below). Each directory has its fans. You will probably want a campground directory for your RV rental adventure. You don't need more than one. Our suggestion is to go someplace, probably an RV dealer or RV supply store, where you can look at both directories and choose the one which most appeals to you. For what it's worth, our personal favorite is the* **"Trailer Life Directory"**, *but we carry both in our RV.*

Woodall's

"The Original Complete Guide to Campgrounds, RV Parks, Service Centers & Attractions." **"Woodall's"** *is available as both a "big book" which covers all of North America and as a series of regional guides. If you decide to use* **"Woodall's"** *as your campground guide, we recommend you get the big book. It isn't that much more expensive and you'll be amazed how much fun it can be to look up campground options in distant locations.*

The Complete Idiot's Guide to RVing
Brent Peterson

"Get in the drivers seat and discover the RV lifestyle." The Idiot's books, and for that matter the Dummies books, have been successful because they do a good job of presenting basic information in an understandable format. This book is about 400 pages and is arguably the best introduction to RVing available today.

Frommer's Exploring America by RV
Shirley Slater & Harry Basch

"Ten Unforgettable Trips, plus Everything You Need to Know to Buy or Rent an RV." This is a book which has received mixed reviews, but is one of our favorites. There is little we enjoy more than traveling by RV . . . and when we're not traveling by RV we like thinking about traveling by RV. With its ten RV Adventures, this book provides plenty of food for thought. We like that a lot. NOTE: At least one reviewer tells us this is exactly *the same book as "***RV Vacations for Dummies***".*

RV and Car Camping Vacations in Europe
Mike and Terri Church

If the idea of an RVing vacation in Europe sounds like something you'd like to explore, this book – and **"European Camping"***, by the same authors – are essential additions to your research library. For more information, go to* www.RollingHomes.com.

Great RV Trips
Charles L Cadieux

"A Guide to the Best RV Trips in the United states, Canada and Mexico." This book consists primarily of detailed information on a variety of RV trips. Great vacations often start with a single good idea. Here are presented 13 wonderful ideas for the RV traveler. A terrific book – both as a planning aid and as arm-chair adventure.

Great Eastern RV Trips
Gordon Groene and Janet Groene

"A Year-Round Guide to the Best RVing in the East." 20 of the best RV vacations from Florida to Canada. Five RV travel ideas are presented for each of the seasons and include some marvelous possibilities for travel in the "shoulder seasons" – when both RV rental rates and crowds are low.

Great Western RV Trips
Jan Bannan
"A Year-Round Guide to the best RVing in the West." The western counterpart of the book above.

RV Repair & Maintenance Manual
Bob Livingston
"The Complete Technical Manual and Troubleshooting Guide." The first choice is for you to have an enjoyable, trouble free RV rental vacation. A close second would be to deal with any problems which arise quickly, efficiently and with no interruptions in your travel plans. This book can't guarantee a vacation free of mechanical challenges, but it can help you to deal with the peculiarities of the operating systems found in your home on wheels.

Complete Guide to Full-Time RVing
Bill and Jan Moeller
"Life on the Open Road." There may come a time on your RV rental vacation when you find yourself wondering what it would be like to just keep on going . . . and going . . . and going. Hundreds of thousands of North Americans have chucked the conventional "sticks and bricks" lifestyle for a life of freedom on the open road. They live and travel in their RVs full-time. If you'd like to learn how they do it, this is the book for you!

Web Resources

General Resources:

The **Go Rving** website, www.gorving.com provides a good, general introduction to RVs and to the RVing lifestyle.

As you begin your search for an RV rental dealer, two good sources of dealer names are the **Recreational Vehicle Rental Association**: www.rvra.org, and the **RV Dealers Association:** www.rvda.org.

Forums:
Internet forums are some of our favorite places to gather RV information. You can either sort through the topics for items of interest or post questions of your own. Three of our favorite forums are

The Open Roads Forum: www.rv.net
The iRV2 Community: www.irv2.com
And the Escapees Forum (in the Members Section): www.escapees.com

RV Tours, Caravans and Rallies:

Many find joining an organized RV caravan, tour or rally is an ideal, low-hassle way to get the most out of their RVing time. And, if an RV trip to Mexico sounds like the thing you are looking for, know that most RV rental firms only allow their units into Mexico as part of an organized caravan. In North America, few of the package tours include a rental RV. Generally, overseas tours offered by the companies listed below include a rental RV in the base tour price. We have not had personal experience with any of the following companies, but all are considered reputable.

Adventure Caravans: www.adventurecaravans.com
Creative World RV Rallies & Caravans: www.creativeworldtravel.com
Fantasy RV Tours: fantasyrvtours.com
Tracks RV Tours: www.trackstoadventure.com
Overseas Motorhome Tours, Inc. www.omtinc.com
European Motorhome Tours: www.rvtoureurope.com

Other Recommendations:

RV Education 101: www.rveducation101.com. *Here you will find a wide range of educational offerings for the RVer – books, e-books, training videos, travel videos and much, much more. A site worth visiting!!*

Great RV Adventures: www.pvptravel.com *This company offers five videos each covering RV travel to a general area. If any of their featured adventures is an area you are even considering for your RV rental vacation, we would list the related video as a "must have" purchase.*

RV Bookstore: www.rvbookstore.com. *Here you will find "the world's biggest and best selection of books, eBooks, videos, DVDs and magazines about recreational vehicles and the RV lifestyle." What more can we say. If it's about the RV lifestyle, you can find it here.*

Your Campsite is Waiting!

Index

W-X-Y-Z

Printed in the United States
60140LVS00004B/87-90